A Complete Guide to Writing for Publication

Susan Titus Osborn,
General Editor

A Complete Guide to Writing for Publication

Susan Titus Osborn,
General Editor

ACW Press
5501 N. 7th Ave. #502
Phoenix, AZ 85013

A Complete Guide to Writing for Publication

Cover design by Eric Walljasper
Page design by Prelude to Print

Publisher's Cataloging-in-Publication
(Provided by Quality Books, Inc.)

A complete guide to writing for publication / [by
Susan Titus Osborn ... et al.]; edited by Susan
Titus Osborn.—1st ed.
p. cm.
Includes bibliographical references
ISBN 1-892525-09-7

1. Authorship. 2. Christian literature—Authorship.
I. Osborn, Susan Titus

PN145.C66 1999 808'.02
QBI99-26

Printed in the United States of America
by Bethany Press International
Bloomington, Minnesota

Contents

Foreword

It's all here, you fortunate people. All the things I had to learn the hard way as an aspiring writer are now spelled out for you by qualified professionals. The question remains: Is your appetite healthy enough to digest the lessons that are so effectively taught in these pages by fellow Christians who sincerely want to help you? In other words, when your computer's switch is turned on, will you be willing to apply what you have learned herein?

Just for fun, and especially for the aspirants, let me shake some of it down into terse, Anglo-Saxon prose:

Sell it, then write it.

Have it critiqued. Then do it over until you are (for the moment) sick of it.

Turn off the machine and go out and find a crowd of writers, editors, and booksellers. Join them, but don't talk. Listen.

Spend a lot of time helping other writers, young and old. You'll be the one blessed.

Don't argue with your editor.

Write for Jesus.

And may God grant to you the "golden needle" of creativity that Jack Cavanaugh describes in his chapter. May it stab your copy with excitement, sparkle, wisdom, joy, and above all, truth.

DR. SHERWOOD E. WIRT
Editor emeritus, *Decision*

— 1 —

Where to Begin

SUSAN TITUS OSBORN

One's mind, once stretched by a new idea,
never regains its original dimensions.
—OLIVER WENDELL HOLMES

PEOPLE OFTEN ASK ME IF THEY have enough talent to write. It is my experience after twenty years of writing, editing, and teaching that talent plays a minor role in the writing process. Writing is mostly hard work. Finding an idea, developing an outline, and writing the rough draft are the easy steps. The difficult part is rewriting, rewriting, and rewriting—polishing your manuscript until it is the best you are capable of writing.

We live in an electronic age of TV, videos, and computers where we obtain things instantaneously. We have instant tea, minute breakfast, fast-food lunches, and microwavable dinners. We expect knowledge and information to come instantly too. However, writing is not instantaneous. It requires time, thought, and commitment.

James Michener once said, "I have never thought of myself as a good writer. Anyone who wants reassurance of that should read one of my first drafts. But I'm one of the world's great rewriters."

Crafting articles, stories, and books is hard work. God doesn't sit at the typewriter or computer for us, but He does provide us with intelligence and abilities. He expects us to use these tools to glorify Him.

Why do you write? Is it to share your story with others? Are you seeking personal growth? Is it a ministry? Is it to make money? Making a living as a freelance writer is extremely difficult. Hopefully, your *main* purpose for writing is to provide a ministry. Personally, I want to change lives and to share something with others that will benefit them. I want my readers to grow closer to God.

What time commitment you are willing to give to your writing? Be aware that you can't wait until everything else is taken care of to sit down at the computer. Writing must be a priority, and it is demanding. You will have to sacrifice other things.

Another important point is to pray for God's guidance before you start writing. We must listen to God and submit to His will before we can write for Him effectively.

Three-Step Writing Process

First Step

Before you begin to write your article or story, decide what your primary purpose is. The first step in the writing process is to state your theme in one word. Then state it in one sentence. Do this for short pieces and devotionals, for stories and articles, as well as for books. Each point of your manuscript must support the main theme.

Another way to look at this point is to say that your article or story must have focus. Georgianna Walker has an excellent definition: "Focus is deciding on a general theme or premise and developing it throughout the piece." Do not deviate from your premise. Doing so is the main problem with the majority of articles that are rejected. The writer tries to tell too many stories in one article.

Next, create a preliminary outline before you write one word of your manuscript. After your outline is complete, finish the first stage of writing your article which is to develop your idea into a full page. This is accomplished by using the analytical, or critical, side of your brain.

An alternative to creating an outline is to use the wheel method. Draw a circle in the middle of a page and write your theme in the center. Draw spokes emanating from the circle, and write concise thoughts about your theme. Do this in any order that your thoughts come. After formulating as many thoughts about your main theme as you can, arrange those thoughts in logical order to form an outline.

Second Step

Wait a few days before you begin the second step of the writing process which is to write the first rough draft. As you begin, let the theme and supporting ideas form in your mind.

Now write your story. Turn off the critical side of your brain, and turn on the creative side. Let the words flow onto the paper. Don't get hung up on spelling, punctuation, or phraseology; just write whatever comes to mind. Try not to think about your outline or theme sentence. Write the first draft in one sitting. Pick a location and time to write that will allow for a minimum of interruptions. Get everything down on paper you can think of regarding your subject. You may end up with enough material for several articles, but don't worry about that when you are writing this first draft.

Writing the first draft is the creative part. For me, this is the easiest part. The hard part is rewriting, rewriting, and rewriting. What separates those who become published writers from those who would like to have written is a willingness to work through this process of polishing their work step-by-step. Your first stories, articles, or books may take a long time; but you will learn from practice. Even if it takes 100 hours to write your first article, it is not wasted time. You will learn valuable lessons to apply to future writing, which should flow more smoothly.

After you have written your first draft, set it aside again for a week or two. It is easy to become so enthused about your first draft that you are convinced it is ready for publication.

Third Step

When you pick up your manuscript for the third time, you've put some distance between your emotions and your work; and you are ready to begin the third step of the writing process. This involves editing your own work. Now you should be able to look at it more objectively. Hopefully you can treat it like a jigsaw puzzle, rearranging some of the pieces to fit better.

First read through it for an overview. Make a mark in the margin where it doesn't flow smoothly. Read quickly. Don't stop and ponder what is wrong. That will come later when you do the line-by-line editing.

Then go back and look at your outline and theme sentence. Do they need revision? Does your article or story support your outline and theme? If not, you need to change either your theme and outline or your first rough draft. Remember, neither is set in concrete.

Now look at the opening sentence and paragraph. Do you have a strong hook? Does the reader want to keep reading? Beginnings, for me, are the most difficult part of a manuscript to write. Often I end up throwing out the first three paragraphs or even the first page. Don't struggle too long on your beginning at this point. You can always come back and edit it on subsequent drafts. Or you may prefer to start with the middle and go back to write the beginning later.

The next step is to carefully go through your article, looking for spelling errors, missing punctuation, and incorrect grammar usage. Tighten your writing. Eliminate unnecessary words. Rearrange the paragraphs and sentences to make it flow smoothly. A good rule of thumb on the comma is to use it when it sounds necessary. Your ear is an excellent guide. Read William Strunk Jr. and E. B. White's book *The Elements of Style* to learn the mechanics of grammar, punctuation, and word usage.

Research

Research is the process of gathering material from a wide variety of sources. Your writing should reflect a great deal of research, so you write with an abundance of material. Hopefully you will develop far more knowledge on a subject than you will need to include in an article or book.

Some books and articles take a great deal of research; others draw more on your own personal experiences. Whether you're writing fiction or nonfiction, however, become knowledgeable on your subject. It is vital to get your facts right and to have every detail accurate. You can lose your credibility with your readers if they find a silly mistake. In the working manuscript of my book *You Start with One*, I had alligators sunning themselves on the riverbank. A biologist informed me that there are no alligators in Sri Lanka. I changed it to crocodiles before the book went to press.

Primary Research

Primary research is information you obtain directly from people, places, or events. This type of research is valuable because it draws you in and makes you, the author, personally involved.

People are wonderful resources, and they are usually willing to help an author. Call scientists, policemen, doctors, and professors—experts in whatever field you are writing. Go to your locations, and walk where you have your main character walk. Talk to people who have been through a similar experience. Find as many sources as time permits.

Secondary Research

Secondary research depends on the printed research found in books, magazines, newspapers, libraries, and museums. A word of caution: Errors can creep in when you depend on others to do your research for you, particularly when you quote someone who is quoting from another source. Sometimes, however, secondary research is your only option or is necessary to supplement your primary research; and there are many valuable sources. Research librarians can become your best friends. *Readers' Guide to Periodical Literature*, *Poole's Index to Periodical Literature*, *National Geographic*, and *The New York Times* on microfiche or online are excellent resources. Encyclopedias are now available online and on CD-ROMs. Online services are invaluable. America Online, CompuServe, and the Worldwide Web offer seemingly infinite sources. Get a modem, and learn how to use these indispensable services. (See chapter 7 for more information on Internet research.)

THE QUERY LETTER

Many editors prefer receiving a query letter rather than the entire manuscript. A query letter is a letter of inquiry asking if a publication would like to see a completed article on a specific subject. Make your letter professional, to the point, and short. Keep it one page in length if possible.

A query letter should answer four questions: (1) Why are you qualified to write the article? (2) What is the article about? (3) Who is your audience? and (4) Why will this article interest the reader?

You can determine whether a publication wants to receive a query or the entire manuscript by checking Sally Stuart's *Christian Writers' Market Guide*. If a periodical wants your entire manuscript, still include a cover letter that contains the same points as a good query letter so the editor can use it for quick reference.

Fiction pieces, poetry, shorts and fillers, and most children's stories usually do not require a query letter. Many magazine editors, however, will want a query instead of the entire manuscript. Even if they want the entire article, write a good cover letter to grab the editor.

There is a good chance an editor will ask for your entire manuscript if you write a quality query letter. When he does, write "requested material" on the outside of your mailing envelope. Always include a postcard so the editor can tell you if he is interested in your article or not.

Manuscript Submission

Once you have polished your manuscript and written it to the best of your ability, have other writers or a professional critique service critique it for you. Details on the Christian Communicator Manuscript Critique Service, which I direct, are at the back of this book.

Format

When you are ready to type your article in final form and send it to a publishing house, use the following format. Your manuscript should be double-spaced on white, 20 pound bond paper with 1 inch margins all around. It is permissible to use computer or photocopy paper, but send a *clean* copy. Use a 12 point Times Roman, Times New Roman, Courier, or Courier New font; and leave the right margin unjustified (ragged). Usually the preset standard margins in a computer word processing program are acceptable as is the default font. Put a heading on each page, and number each page.

Left Heading

Always put your name, address, and telephone number in the top left corner of the first page of the manuscript. If an editor needs to call you, he has your phone number at his fingertips.

Right Heading

To maintain balance, these are the four items that go in the top right corner of the first page.

1. *Rights:* On the first line, list the rights you are offering. Normally if this is the first time you are selling your article or story, you will offer first rights. This gives an editor one-time rights to publish your material before you offer it to another publication. *Do not* offer your article or story elsewhere until after it comes out in print if you sold first rights.

Once your article or story is printed by the publication to which you first sold it, then you may sell second or reprint rights. Copies of this same manuscript can be sent simultaneously to many different publications, but make sure they don't have overlapping audiences.

2. *Word count:* On the second line, write the approximate number of words. If your article or story is over 500 words, round off to the nearest 100 words. If it is a filler under 500 words, estimate to the nearest 50 words. Most word processing programs have a word count built in.

3. *Copyright:* The third line is for your copyright information. Most computer programs allow you to insert a copyright symbol into the text. Also include the year and your legal name.

4. *Social Security number:* Your Social Security number goes on the fourth line. A publisher cannot pay you unless he has your Social Security number. Your check may be delayed if an editor has to ask you for this number at a later date.

Subsequent Pages

Use a header with your last name and a key word from the title in the top left corner of the second and all following pages. Put the page number in the top right corner of all but the first page.

Mailing

Make a second hard copy of your manuscript. Also back up the computer hard disk copy of your article on a floppy disk. Computers can crash and take all your information with them. Never mail the only copy of your article or story, and never fold a manuscript. Place it in a 9" x 12" envelope. Include another folded 9" x 12", self-addressed, stamped envelope (SASE) if you want your manuscript returned; or include a self-addressed, stamped postcard if you don't. Before you mail your manuscript, make a list of all the publishing houses that might consider buying it.

Mail your manuscript to a specific editor, not just to a publishing house. If you've met an editor at a writers' conference, it helps considerably. Mention that person by name in your cover or query letter.

Remember, God uses ordinary people to do extraordinary things. He will use us if we listen to Him and then go out and give 150 percent of ourselves to what He has asked us to do.

People in today's microwavable society are searching for meaning in their lives. America is hungry for spiritual fulfillment. We can meet their needs with the power of our pens. However, our thoughts, ideas, and words need to reflect His thoughts. So write with love and emotion. Write quality stories and articles. Write what Jesus would write if He held your pen in His hand.

Susan Titus Osborn directs the Christian Communicator Manuscript Critique Service and is a contributing editor for *The Christian Communicator* and *The Galilean*. Susan is also an adjunct professor at Pacific Christian College of Hope International University in Fullerton, California. She has authored eighteen books and numerous articles, devotionals, and curriculum materials and is a publisher's representative for Broadman & Holman Publishers. She has taught at over 110 writers' conferences across the United States and in five foreign countries. She is listed in *Who's Who of American Women, Who's Who in the World, Who's Who in the West, and Who's Who in the Media and Communications*. For information on the Christian Communicator Manuscript Critique Service and her six session e-mail course contact Susan at 3133 Puente Street, Fullerton, CA 92835; phone: 714-990-1532; e-mail: Susanosb@aol.com; Web site: www.christiancommunicator.com.

2

Writing Articles That Sell and Touch Lives

MARLENE BAGNULL

Write my answer on a billboard, large and clear, so that anyone can read it at a glance and rush to tell the others.
—HABAKKUK 2:2, TLB

HAD IT NOT BEEN FOR THE through-the-Bible-in-a-year plan I was following, I might never have read the above words of this minor prophet. These words have since made a major impact on my life as I have sought to be faithful to the strong sense of God's call despite my "Who, me?" doubts.

To some it may seem audacious to attempt to write God's answer to the complex problems facing men and women, boys and girls, as we prepare to enter a new millennium. In our own strength, it would indeed be audacious; but He has promised: "Now you have every grace and blessing; every spiritual gift and power for doing his will are yours during this time of waiting for the return of our Lord Jesus Christ" (1 Corinthians 1:7, TLB).

During the last several decades, Christian publishing and opportunities for would-be writers of both fiction and nonfiction have grown at a phenomenal rate. While I love to read fiction, I've always found myself drawn to write nonfiction articles. Why? Perhaps, at first, because I believed the grade school teacher who told me I lacked creativity and imagination. Forty plus years and over a thousand sales later of primarily articles and devotionals, I know I believed a lie. Articles also require creativity and imagination and so much more if we are to effectively write His answer.

Evaluate Your Idea

When I first started writing, I worried that I'd run out of ideas. Snatching whatever was at hand, including my children's homework papers, I taught myself to immediately capture the idea on paper. Conscientiously, I maintained a file drawer full of ideas, believing Dr. James Dobson's statement that creativity is linked to retrievability. The truth is, however, that many of my ideas have not merited developing.

How can you and I insure that our articles are worth the trees cut down to make the paper they will be printed on? Same as Habakkuk. We need to "wait to see what answer God will give" (2:1, TLB) for it is God's answer, not ours, that has the power to change lives.

Another way to evaluate which ideas should never see the light of day is to ask who, what, when, where, and why.

Who will read it? It's critically important that we know to whom we are writing. Is the audience male or female, single or married, young or old? If we're writing to children or teens, are we with this age group frequently enough to understand how they think? If we're writing to adults, do we share the same basic beliefs? Writing to convert the editor and his readership to our way of thinking seldom does more than create alienation.

What do we have to say? Has is been said before? If so, can we say it in a fresh, new way? Do we have a clear purpose for writing this? If we don't know where we're going, we're likely never to get there.

When? Is it timely? One of my favorite Hagar cartoons shows three things necessary for victory; but the most important of these, as the drawbridge goes up, is timing. We also need to know the lead time of the periodical where we plan to submit the article and to think seasonally.

Where? We need to know which billboard is publishing what God is calling us to write. Here's where the importance of market research cannot be underestimated.

Finally, *why?* Will the article meet a universal need? Is there, as Wightman Weese taught me, a transferable truth? The editors of *Decision* call this the "take-away factor." Another way to look at this is to ask ourselves, "So what?" What difference will this make?

SHARPEN YOUR FOCUS

One of the major problems in the manuscripts I read (and often in my own manuscripts before they go through needed rewrites) is the lack of a sharp focus. Jim Watkins, in *The Persuasive Person*, compares this problem to sitting through a missionary slide show when the slides are not quite in focus. Since our readers are not a captive audience and have no compunction against getting up and leaving, we're going to lose them unless we make our message "large and clear" (Habbakuk 2:2, TLB).

"You need to condense your idea to one sentence," Lee Roddy told me years ago. And because he knew I have a problem with wordiness, he took away my commas and semicolons. It was valuable advice that I've taken to heart. Posting that sentence above my computer helps me to stay on target and to avoid tangents that are best reserved for another article or a sidebar.

CHOOSE THE BEST TYPE

Knowing what kind of article can best present what we want to say and making certain the magazine where we plan to submit it takes this kind of article is an important key to getting our work in print. Let's look at some of the most salable types of articles.

Devotional, Inspirational, and Personal Experience

These types of articles must touch and move the reader. As Dina Donohue, a former editor of *Guideposts*, said, "They need to create heart-tug." Remember that the purpose of these types of articles is to inspire, not preach or teach.

Self-help

Have you been through some hard places and lived/learned enough to see the other side? These times when God has had you on the growing edge provide a wonderful opportunity for ministering to the needs of your readers. Be sure to provide practical, workable, realistic solutions and to avoid pat, simplistic answers.

How-to

Are there things you know well enough to teach someone else? Keep in mind that it's difficult to write on familiar topics, such as prayer and the importance of a daily quiet time. Unless you have something new and unique to add to what has already been said, it is better to steer to a topic that is not so overworked. Realize, too, that time spent in research and interviewing the experts can transform a ho-hum how-to article into an outstanding one that your readers will clip and refer to repeatedly.

Marriage and Family Living

Bill Keene's Family Circus cartoons have often caused me to chuckle and to think. Why? Because he addresses real life. As Christian writers we need to do the same. Presenting a phony, this-is-how-it-should-be or how-I-would-like-it-to-be picture creates guilt trips, not solutions. Today's families are stretched and stressed, and Christians are not immune from the pain of divorce. Articles that present biblical truth with sensitivity and compassion are needed and will be published.

Biblical Teaching

While the market for in-depth biblical teaching articles is limited, we must not let this discourage us from writing them. I am convinced that the doors of publication will open when we show the relevancy of God's Word to the topic being addressed, when the article is finely crafted, and when we are in tune theologically with the magazine. In order to write biblical teaching articles, we must make a commitment to be "a workman…who correctly handles the word of truth" (2 Timothy 2:15). Not only does this mean we cannot proof text or take passages out of context, it is also critically important that we quote accurately. There is no room for carelessness in the handling of God's Word.

Opinion Pieces and Editorials

In recent years, Judeo-Christian standards have increasingly come under attack by social engineers who are working to create an "anything goes" society. We need to combat this slide down the slippery slope by accepting the invitation of the Amy Writing Awards to present biblical truth in secular, nonreligious publications. I especially want to encourage you not to overlook the most-read section of your hometown newspaper, the editorial page.

CREATE STRONG READER IDENTIFICATION

"Have we walked a mile in the moccasins of our readers?" a paraphrased Native American proverb asks us. Have we made this empathy obvious to our readers? In other words, if we cannot convince our readers that we know and understand their daily struggles, our words will not carry the credibility needed to make a difference in their lives. Indeed, our readers are likely not to even finish articles no matter how well it is crafted or how wise our words may be.

We need to know and to be able to picture our readers if we hope to connect with them. What would we say to them, and they to us, if we were to sit down together over a cup of coffee? Would there be awkward pauses because we do not have anything in common and do not speak the same language of life experience? Or would we be able to look deeply into one another's eyes and begin to share, openly and honestly, about things that really matter?

Our willingness to be vulnerable as well as writing in a conversational tone will go a long way to creating reader identification. Humor is another way to connect with our readers and to reach their hearts so they "will rush to tell the others" (Habakkuk 2:2, TLB) how our article has spoken to them.

DEVELOP A SOUND STRUCTURE

A structurally weak and disorganized manuscript is likely to be returned no matter how intriguing the idea may be. The fact is, editors simply don't have time to untangle our muddled thoughts nor to do our work for us.

Sherwood Wirt, editor emeritus of *Decision*, said in a workshop, "We need to get into the business of outlining, but don't let it show. The skeleton must never show, any more than it does in our bodies. We clothe it with flesh, but the basic skeleton must be there."

If you are one of those writers who says, "Ugh," at the thought of outlining an article despite the new outline features of popular word processors, let me suggest some alternatives that will enable your readers at a glance to grasp your point and follow your thinking through to your conclusion.

Index cards, Post-it** Notes, and the cut-and-paste features of your word processor are great ways to capture the main points of your article and to spread them out and move them around until they flow in a logical order.

The "train technique" presented by Omer Henry in *Writing and Selling Magazine Articles* begins with the cowcatcher clearing the track through the use of a strong lead that grabs the reader's attention. The locomotive is the power thrust of the article and contains the focus statement. The cars are your points, but don't make this a long freight train! Finally, the caboose is your conclusion. I remember how cheated I felt as a youngster when I'd sit at a railroad crossing waiting for a train to pass and the caboose was missing. This technique visually reminds me not to cheat my readers by failing to wrap up my article with a strong conclusion.

"Hey! You! See! So?" described by Walter Campbell in his book *Writing Nonfiction* works well for many writers. "Hey!" is your lead, also called the hook, where you have about five seconds to grab your readers' attention and compel them to read on. "You!" is your focus statement or—another way of putting it—your what's-in-it-for-me-the-reader statement. "See!" is the body of your article with the points you want to make. Too many and you'll overwhelm your reader. Too few and your treatment of the topic will be considered shallow. And "So?" is your conclusion and take-away.

Write, Rewrite, and Edit

Someone once said, "I'm not a writer, I'm a rewriter!" I find writers tend to be weak in the area of editing, perhaps because they think it is the editor's job. It's easy to become overwhelmed by all the things that need to be incorporated into our articles and checked and double checked if we want to make a good impression on an editor.

Because of this situation, I developed a writer's check-off list over twenty years ago. On it I included such items as smooth transitions, varying sentence and paragraph length, checking for inconsistencies in capitalization and punctuation, avoiding qualifiers, double checking the accuracy of all quotes and statistics, and adding the fiction technique of "show don't tell" as well as anecdotes. Bringing my check-off list into the computer age, I've added: Use grammar and spell checkers cautiously. I'll always be grateful for the editor who caught, and added, the missing word left out of my introduction to *My Turn to Care: Affirmations for Caregivers of Aging Parents* so it correctly reads: "This I know...he will not abandon us."

DO YOUR MARKET RESEARCH

Years ago, in a workshop at the St. Davids Christian Writers Conference, Ruth Peterman said she spent an almost equal time researching the markets as she did writing. I was horrified. It all sounded so crass. After all, I wanted my writing to be a ministry. But I've learned that Ruth was right.

Market research is a step that cannot be overlooked if we want our articles to sell and touch lives. With the topical indexes in Sally Stuart's *Christian Writers' Market Guide* and her columns in *The Christian Communicator* and *Advanced Christian Writer,* we have no excuse for incorrectly targeting our articles. If we ignore these resources and fail to send for sample copies and writers' guidelines before submitting our manuscripts, we brand ourselves as careless amateurs and hurt other Christian writers by causing doors to close for freelance material.

The journey to publication of the articles we believe God is calling us to write can often be long and discouraging. But have faith! He who calls us to write His answer also promises: "Slowly, steadily, surely, the time approaches when the vision will be fulfilled. If it seems slow, do not despair, for these things will surely come to pass. Just be patient! They will not be overdue a single day!" (Habakkuk 2:3, TLB).

MARLENE BAGNULL has made over a thousand sales to Christian periodicals and is the author of six books, including the new, expanded version of *Write His Answer: A Bible Study for Christian Writers* (ACW Press).

Marlene is the founder and director of the Greater Philadelphia Christian Writers Conference. She also directs the Colorado Christian Writers Conference, speaks at Christian writers' conferences around the nation, gives one- and two-day Write His Answer seminars, and teaches a correspondence study program for Christian writers called the At-Home Writing Workshops. You may reach her at 316 Blanchard Road, Drexel Hill, PA 19026 or via e-mail at mbagnull@aol.com.

— 3 —

Edit Yourself before Someone Else Does It for You

JULIE-ALLYSON IERON

In composing, as a general rule, run a pen through every other word you have written; you have no idea what vigor it will give your style.

—SYDNEY SMITH

RED INK. THERE'S SOMETHING repulsive about it—especially when it's running like a river in flood stage all over our freshly written literary masterpieces. We're conditioned to dread red ink. In financial circles, it means our cash flow is in the negative column, our accounts are overdrawn, and our income is insufficient to cover our outlay. In writing circles, red ink means an editor considers our literary deposit overdrawn. Our work is insufficient to cover the great expectations we had for it.

Who among us can't recall the heart-sinking feeling of having an article returned smeared with the dreaded red ink? In neon lights, the hot color called attention to the fact that the assignment was deficient. When this has happened to me, I have felt devalued—as though not only my work, but I personally, don't measure up. So I have learned some techniques that help me avoid red ink—or at least limit its appearance on my manuscripts.

MAKE TIME TO EDIT

Just as accurate budgeting can keep my financial statements in the black, budgeting a portion of my writing time for self-editing can accomplish the same objective. As general editor and primary writer of the *Believer's Life System Women's Edition*, I often have a platform from which to speak on the principles of time management that have worked for me for many years. All of the principles I teach hinge on one simple fact: If something is truly important to us, we *will* find time to do it.

In my writing, I consider it important to submit a polished manuscript to my publisher—whether it is a newspaper story, a magazine article, or a full-length book. I don't do this just to avoid red ink (although that is part of my motivation), but because my reputation as a thorough, efficient writer depends on the finished quality of my work. I've been on both the writing and editing sides of publishing, and I know how much publishers value writers whose work requires little revision. In fact, there have been times when I was working for a small publication where I was both writer and editor. These roles are difficult, but not impossible, to fulfill simultaneously if: (1) as "writer" I am careful to hold myself to high standards of writing quality; and (2) as "editor," I am ruthless with my pruning shears.

When I was writing my first book, *Names of Women of the Bible*, I had an extremely tight schedule. The publisher gave me just five months to research and write the stories of fifty-two women from the Bible, making them come alive to readers in our post-Christian culture. All of this was in addition to my full-time work and travel schedule with the *Believer's Life System*.

I had five months of Saturdays, Sundays, and holidays in which to write a 50,000-word book. So I planned and maintained an aggressive schedule that would leave three weekends for final polishing at the end of the five months. Polishing my manuscript was important to me; so even on such a short timetable, I planned ahead to allow time for it.

The result was worth the extra effort. Aside from a few minor details on the footnotes, the editor was pleased with the thoroughness of the manuscript. She was able to do her work quickly and efficiently because I had done mine the same way.

Don the Editor's Hat

The process of editing is a separate and distinct entity from the process of writing. It requires different skills. Self-editing requires that you be detached emotionally from the piece you have created.

You cannot be a good editor while you are still enamored with your own words. I like to let a completed manuscript simmer for a few days (or in the case of my book a few weeks), so I can begin to look at the work with fresh, critical eyes.

I liken this shift in perspective to the changing of a hat. I have a goofy hat that I sometimes wear when I write. It features a little, purple Disney character named Figment (as in figment of the imagination). I consider this my creative hat. But I take off this hat when it comes to editing. In my mind, I don one of those shabby newspaper reporters' fedoras from a bygone era. And with it, I don the crusty attitude of the old-fashioned news room: If it doesn't fit, chop it off. If it isn't clear and simple, make it so. If it doesn't make deadline, it doesn't get in print.

Perhaps it would help to clarify what a modern-day editor looks for in a polished, complete manuscript. Of course, if it has been written on assignment, it must be on time. It should be laid out with sufficient margins and adequate spacing in a clear typeface—not a specialty font or colorful type. (This may sound unbelievable, but just a few years ago I received a handwritten article submission for the magazine I was managing. The writer had used purple ink on pink flowery stationery. That article never had a chance of making it into print.)

The manuscript should appear clean (no ketchup, grease, or coffee stains) and be free of typographical, spelling, and grammatical errors. These days, our word processing programs can do much of this grunt work for us. So there's absolutely no excuse for sloppiness in our finished manuscripts.

But editors look for much more than cleanliness, timeliness, and legibility as they consider a manuscript for publication. In a word, they look for writing that is focused.

Focus on Your Audience

Nothing is more frustrating to me as an editor than to receive article submissions that are mismatched for my magazine or publishing house. Any writer who wishes to freelance for a publication must take the time to become familiar with it. For a book publisher, that means knowing their catalog and understanding their niche in the publishing world. For a magazine, that means reading several recent issues, the writers' guidelines, and the upcoming theme lists (if available) to be sure you are pitching the right article (with the right angle) to the right publication.

For example, recently, I was invited to write articles on time management for three different publications. For a student magazine, I focused on how to manage academic schedules, making time for a social life, and minimizing the necessity of all-nighters. For a general-interest Christian magazine, I focused on stories about how I began aligning my life by God's priority system, looking at Jesus' example. For a writers' journal, I keyed in on how I make time for a freelancing career while working a full-time job. With the same topic, I used different angles for different audiences.

Focus on Tight Writing

More words do not necessarily translate into better communication. Often, in fact, they have the opposite effect. When I teach at writers' workshops, I often throw in a bonus "commercial" for self-editing. On an overhead, I show a book review, submitted by one of my regular reviewers. In 128 words, the writer succeeded in creating such a convoluted paragraph that it took three editors to understand it. After we all had a few chuckles (as I attempted to read the entire review in one breath), I showed the fifty-one-word paragraph as edited. The review needed my machete. So does much of my own writing. Here's what I target for deletion in my pursuit of tight writing.

Redundancies

Writing professor Holly Miller gives her classes a handout that I still keep in my files. It lists dozens of redundant phrases that insidiously invade our vocabulary, such as "foresee the future" (can one foresee the past?), "unintentional accident" (can an accident be intentional?), "connected together" (can something be connected apart?), and "personal opinion" (can an opinion be impersonal?). When we use these phrases in our writing, they add to the word count but detract from meaningful communication.

Clutter Words

Legendary editor Stanley Walker told young writers "to avoid adjectives and to swear by the little verbs that bounce and leap and swim and cut." While carefully chosen adjectives and adverbs do have a place in good writing, their excessive use is a sign of lazy editing. For example: "a lively, colorful, explosive fiesta." Doesn't the word *fiesta* conjure up a lively, colorful, and explosive celebration? Be merciless; delete those adjectives. My rule is: If a sentence communicates the same and flows smoothly without a phrase, then that phrase must go. Here are some phrases that seldom add any meaning: of some kind, kind of, type of, a lot of, and plenty of.

Clichés

Once upon a time clichés were born as fresh ways to describe old concepts. Then they became so common and overused that they no longer communicated. Avoid clichés "like the plague." (Oops! Strike that last phrase.) Instead, let your creativity flow. Find a fresh way to communicate. Who knows? Maybe your newly coined phrase will one day become a cliché.

FOCUS ON KEY POINTS

I recommend writing from an outline—a broad-stroke, here's-where-I'm-going-with-this-piece outline. Read through your notes, then select key points, deciding tentatively in what order they will appear. Next create the lead or introduction that will set the tone. Only then should you begin writing. The outline will provide a yardstick against which to measure the manuscript as you edit. With your editor's hat on, refer to your outline and ask the following questions.

Have I Focused on the Right Points?

This is a question of mission. Reread the lead or introduction to determine what promises you made to the reader at the outset. In Composition 101 we called this contract with the reader our thesis. (It's also wise to use this opportunity to refresh your memory with the promises you made to the publisher.) Even though in popular writing we don't always create a formal thesis, the concept remains the same. When we set up a reader to expect certain things, we want her to find all those things as she reads our work. So do a complete read through of the manuscript to be certain you've delivered what you promised.

Does Everything Fit Neatly into One of Those Key Areas?

Extraneous facts, nice as they might be to know, will just muddy up the piece. When we've spent hours researching, we are tempted to do a "file dump" and cram all of that research into the article. That doesn't impress the reader. Rather, it may confuse him and cause him to stop reading entirely. If, while you're in the editing mode, you identify facts that do not fit neatly into the final manuscript, then you must get out your machete and hack away. One way to handle intriguing, yet extraneous facts is to take them out of the article and place them in a sidebar. This way we can show they are related to the main article, but they don't distract the reader from the key points. Sidebars have the benefit of adding a second entry point to draw a potential reader into the article.

Does the Writing Have an Appropriate Pace and Flow?

Appropriate is the key. We must pace a reader through a manuscript. All the exciting stories ought not be clumped in one area. Neither should all the statistical data appear in a cluster. Statistics strategically placed can be wonderful support material. If they are clumped together, they will frustrate or bore the reader. Too much excitement at once can be a sensory overload—like an overdone shoot-em-up movie. As you massage your manuscripts into their final form, consider moving material around because of pace considerations. Try to lead off with a strong hook. Keep the readers moving through the manuscript with good information along the way. I think it's crucial, though, to save a surprise or an exciting quote for the end—to keep them reading all the way through.

Joseph Stowell did this masterfully in his book *Interruptions*. He started with a gripping tale of a hostage situation on the campus of Moody Bible Institute (where he is President). Throughout the book, he added facts to the story. Finally, in the last few pages, he described the resolution. Once you started reading, the hunger to know the outcome of this frightening scene kept you intrigued throughout the manuscript.

Does the Manuscript Answer All the Questions Readers Will Have?

Cheap who-dunits and B-grade adventure films are notorious for leaving holes. Too often, the hero escapes at the last moment through a doorway that miraculously appears where none had been before. If the writer has not planted hints of a satisfying plot resolution that an astute viewer might reasonably notice along the way, the ending will seem to be a cop-out created by a bored or rushed writer. These extreme examples illustrate the fact that our own manuscripts need to leave readers feeling that we have answered all their questions.

This point hit home to me after I had turned in an article to *Moody*. The story featured a young couple who teach a teen Bible study in their home. I had included details about the study and about the kids who are clamoring to get into it. But it wasn't until I received an e-mail message from the editor that I realized I had neglected to explain that the couple contacted the parents before inviting kids to join the study. That would have been a major omission in parenting circles.

WHERE DOES IT ALL END?

It is important to note that, as different as they are, editing and writing are processes that can go on in tandem. As I wrote this chapter, for example, I frequently reread sections, adding bits of detail, choosing words that fit more comfortably, and even excising sentences that didn't fit. Few sentences appear in print exactly the way I wrote them the first time. I had initially planned to place this paragraph elsewhere. However, it seemed more appropriate in this position. So I moved it.

One caution is in order. Do not let the endless task of editing overtake you and crowd out the creativity of the writing process. When I read something I have written, I always see words and sentences I wish I had stated differently. There comes a point, however, that I need to stop polishing and release my work into the able hands of a professional editor. It's just like polishing silver. If I don't use enough polish, it still looks tarnished. But if I use more polish than the silver needs, it doesn't produce a good return on my investment of elbow grease.

So edit away. Make every word count. Structure your outline carefully. Pace yourself. And once your manuscript shines like sterling, let it go, so you can be free to conquer new (and even more challenging) writing projects.

Julie-Allyson Ieron has worked as managing editor of Moody Press, general editor of the *Believer's Life System Women's Edition*, and an editor for *Moody*. She is a freelance writer and speaker and director of Joy Media, Inc., in suburban Chicago. Julie is the author of *Names of Women of the Bible* (Moody). You may reach her via e-mail at jieron@aol.com.

— 4 —

Making the Most of Writers' Conferences

Lin Johnson

It's nearly impossible to attend a writer's conference without meeting people who could prove important to your writing career.
—Steven D. and Lee G. Spratt

In a fifteen-minute appointment, Katherine sold her first manuscript, a children's book, to a publishing house notorious for telling writers to get published elsewhere and then come to them.

Bob discovered his manuscripts kept coming back because he was sending them in the wrong format to the wrong markets.

During a brief elevator ride, Nancy pitched an idea to a magazine editor who bought the finished manuscript she had brought with her.

Neva, with a best-selling book, was so discouraged she was ready to quit writing. But God had another idea and gave her a new direction.

All these incidents happened at writers' conferences to authors who testify that their investments of time and money were invaluable. In today's publishing market, which is closing more and more to unsolicited manuscripts and proposals, attending a conference once a year has become a vital link to getting published. Plus there are other benefits.

Benefits of Attending a Conference

Writing is, for the most part, a solitary activity. But an annual writers' conference can provide the encouragement and motivation we need to start or continue going. Attending a conference provides a day or a week with other writers who understand us and what we do.

No matter what stage your writing career is at, a conference is a means to improve your writing, editing, and marketing skills; to learn about new markets; and to find out what editors do and do not want right now. It's also the best place to network with both editors and writers. At conferences, I've learned about markets to avoid because of how editors treat writers, picked up tips for future projects, and sold manuscripts.

One of the most important benefits of attending a conference is meeting editors. No matter what type of writing you do, knowing editors will boost your sales. In the book field, more and more publishers are refusing to take unsolicited proposals through the mail. In order for writers to get a foot in the door, they have to do one of three things: submit their proposals through *The Writers Edge*, a clearinghouse for book proposals (P.O. Box 1266, Wheaton, IL 60189); join *First Edition* on the Evangelical Christian Publishers Association Web page (www.ecpa.org); or get to know editors. The latter method is more effective, and attending conferences are usually the best way to meet those editors.

Choosing a Conference

There are more writers' conferences today from which to choose than ever before. So how do you decide which one to attend? For a complete listing of Christian conferences, see the conference section in the back of the *Christian Writers' Market Guide* by Sally Stuart. She lists conferences by state along with such basic information as the date, contact person, attendance, and classes for advanced writers. If you're interested in writing for the general market, the May issue of *Writer's Digest* lists conferences by state with contact information. Write or e-mail the directors to get on mailing lists. And don't hesitate to call them for more information about their conferences if it's too early to get brochures.

Before registering for a conference, decide why you want to go. If you want to meet editors and sell your work, check the faculty list to see which editors will be available and whether or not they are from the publications and/or publishing houses in which you are interested. Certainly if you're trying to sell a book proposal, editors will be a key factor in your decision. Be aware that some freelance writers represent houses but can't buy your manuscripts or proposals, however. What they can do is tell you if the acquisitions editor might be interested in seeing your work or if it is not appropriate for that house.

If you are more interested in improving your writing skills, note the classes that are offered. Do they deal with topics in which you need to improve your craft and which will help you expand your skills? If you're a published author or a professional freelancer, are there classes at advanced levels?

If you're also seeking inspiration, check out the plenary speakers. Although they probably won't be the deciding factor for a conference, the general sessions can help to recharge you for another year. Usually directors choose well-known authors as keynote speakers so you may be able to hear and meet one of your favorite writers.

A few conferences offer college credit and/or CEUs so check to see if a conference is connected with a college. If so, you can earn credits toward a degree or fulfill required continuing education for your job.

Another advantage of attending a writers' conference is the opportunity to get your manuscripts critiqued and meet with the critiquer. If you want this kind of one-on-one help, look for a conference that offers this service. It will usually cost you extra but will be worth the price.

Don't overlook the length or size of the conference. Longer ones allow more time to meet with editors. A one- or two-day conference offers a number of class choices to improve your education, but appointment times with faculty members may be limited or nonexistent. If you hate crowds, consider a smaller, one-day conference; but realize you'll trade off the intimacy for a much smaller faculty and limited choices.

Once you've identified conferences that meet your needs, then look at dates and locations. Attending one nearby will be less costly. But you may want to combine one with a vacation, thus allowing you to visit another area of the country (perhaps even take a cruise) and write off a portion of the expenses on your income taxes.

Although cost is something to consider, don't let it be the only factor. Conferences that run for four or five days cost more but also offer more. Think of a conference as an investment in your career. Mary Lou Sather, who has attended the Write-to-Publish Conference for years, told me, "The leads and assignments I've received have always covered all my costs and more." If finances are a problem, some conferences offer work scholarships. Or your church may help you pay the fees.

Preparing for a Conference

Once you've chosen a conference, learn what you can about the publishing houses represented so you can prepare ideas, queries, or proposals targeted for the editors who will be there. Be sure to read the registration letter carefully for information about what to bring and where to go when you arrive.

Study the schedule and tentatively choose your classes, but be prepared for changes due to faculty cancellations. Don't feel like you have to attend everything; allow yourself some down time. If the conference includes manuscript evaluations or the opportunity for paid critiques, take advantage of these features to get feedback on your writing and note the cutoff date for manuscript submissions.

Take some time to write down your questions. Then don't be shy about asking them at appropriate times. Faculty members and other conferees will be glad to help you.

The clothes and amenities you pack will depend on the conference and room accommodations. Since classroom temperatures may vary, plan to wear layers. Be sure to take several copies of your résumé, list of writing credits, and manuscripts to sell (with SASEs) or get evaluated. Also tuck in a few extra SASEs to give to editors for materials you request or to fellow conferees for copies of articles, etc. And don't forget to bring a stack of business cards; comfortable walking shoes; a legal pad or notebook and pens; a briefcase for carrying your notebook and other materials; an extra suitcase or bag for freebies and purchases; and, of course, cash, checks, or a credit card (if taken).

Even though you won't be able to record classes if someone is taping sessions for sale, take a small tape recorder, tapes, and batteries anyway. You never know when you'll meet a good interview subject, and you'll want to be prepared. If you plan to write during the conference, you'll need a laptop computer, power cord, surge protector, disks, and perhaps a portable printer, cable, and paper.

ATTENDING A CONFERENCE

When you attend the conference, go with a teachable spirit and openness to new directions. You never know how God will use a class or conversation to speak directly to you. Plus if you are open to constructive criticism of your manuscripts—instead of becoming defensive—you'll gain much help to improve your writing.

Plan to arrive early enough to allow yourself some time to read the registration materials before the first session begins. Directors try to put most of the orientation information you will need in writing to make your experience a pleasant and profitable one.

As soon as possible, sign up for the allotted number of appointments with faculty members. Remember, they are human, approachable, and not to be feared. Editors attend conferences to find writers and manuscripts, and professional writers were once novices. If you have ideas or manuscripts targeted for specific editors, sign up with them. If not, talk with professional writers. They will be glad to answer your questions, skim your queries and manuscripts to see if they are ready to show to editors, and brainstorm possible markets with you.

If you have manuscripts or proposals to give to editors, be prepared to talk about them. Some editors will ask you to relate your theme and purpose statements and identify your audience verbally rather than reading your manuscript. And since papers can get lost in transit, most editors will ask you to mail your manuscripts or proposals after the conference rather than taking them back to the office with them.

Soon after arriving, collect the free magazine samples, book catalogs, and writers' guidelines that most conferences make available.

Take one of everything, and sort through your stack when you get home. You never know what new markets you will discover that you might have overlooked otherwise.

Most conference directors set up bookstores with large selections of books on writing and related topics as well as books authored by conferees. Be sure to browse the bookstore often and buy books and tapes to expand your library and improve your craft. You may also want to purchase books by conferees and get them autographed to take home to your spouse and children.

If the classes and general sessions are taped, buy tapes for sessions you miss due to appointments, conflicting classes, and time off. Even though it's impossible for directors to provide copies of all the instructors' handouts for every conferee, you can ask individual teachers for their handouts to go with the tapes you buy.

Don't be afraid to ask questions—in appropriate classes, at appointments with faculty members, and at meals. But don't monopolize classes with your questions and arguments about theology; other people came to hear the instructor, not you.

Use this opportunity to make new friends. Even shy, introverted people already have something to talk about at writers' conferences. So walk up to people, introduce yourself, and ask about their writing interests and conference experiences. Find out what houses they've written for and any problems they've had with them. A writers' conference is often the only place you'll be able to compare notes on publishers and find out who to avoid.

Throughout the conference, pace yourself and get enough sleep. Just because the schedule is packed doesn't mean you *have* to attend everything. Give yourself permission to take breaks, go for walks, take naps, read, talk with others, or just goof off.

Even if you are commuting, plan to eat meals with the group to get acquainted with fellow writers and editors, as these are valuable networking times. Instead of eating with the same people, however, look for different conferees and faculty members to join at each meal to broaden your experience.

Then at the end of the conference, take a few minutes to fill out the evaluation form before you leave. Directors take your comments seriously and use them to improve their conferences the following year.

FOLLOWING UP AFTER THE CONFERENCE

When you get home, write thank-you notes to your instructors and the editors you met. Tell them you appreciate their time and advice. And don't forget to include the director, mentioning how the conference benefited you specifically.

Then set aside a few hours to sort through the freebies you picked up, study the ones that interest you, and file away the information. Begin reading the books you purchased, and listen to the tapes. Review your notes, listing a few goals to work toward based on what you learned.

Also be sure to follow through on ideas you discussed with editors by sending queries, proposals, and manuscripts. As an editor, I've approved far more ideas than the writers I've talked with have sent me. What a waste of a selling opportunity to get an editor interested in your idea, then not follow through!

PLANNING FOR THE FUTURE

One writers' conference may not meet all your needs, especially as they change throughout your writing career. Some writers return to the same conference every year because the faculty and classes vary enough each year. Plus they get to see friends they've made there. Other writers prefer to go to different conferences each year. The choice is yours.

But for writers who want to publish, attending writers' conferences is not an option. No longer can we afford *not* to attend on a regular basis.

LIN JOHNSON directs the Write-to-Publish Conference at Wheaton College (Chicago) and teaches at writers' conferences around the world. She is the managing editor of *Advanced Christian Writer* and *Church Libraries* and a freelance editor and writer specializing in Bible curriculum. Lin has written almost sixty books, including *Fighting the Good Fight* and *Standing Firm in Truth* with John Stott (InterVarsity), *Encouraging Others* (Harold Shaw), *Our Good Provider* (Zondervan), *Teaching Junior Highers* (Accent), and *Christian Education: Foundations for the Future*

(Moody). Plus she has contributed to several other books. Lin is a Gold Medallion Book Award recipient. You may reach her by e-mail at lin-johnson@compuserve.com.

— 5 —

I Am a Writer: The Marks of a Professional

GAYLE G. ROPER

Writing is easy. All you do is sit staring at a blank sheet of paper until the drops of blood form on your forehead.

—GENE FOWLER

HAVE YOU MADE THE GREAT decision that all writers have to make some time or another? What is this momentous choice, you ask? It's the determination to declare that you are a professional writer, not merely a hobbyist.

There are three reasons to make this decision. One has to do with the way you perceive yourself and your mission. The second has to do with the IRS and the way you will henceforth deal with this agency. The third flows from one and two and touches on the thoroughness of your record keeping.

YOU AND YOUR MISSION

When I began writing almost thirty years ago, I began on the kitchen table during my kids' naps, typing on my old college portable typewriter. I was a hobbyist. I was having fun, using my mind in a way I didn't when I mopped, dusted, cleaned the toilets, and tried to teach table manners to two little boys who loved emulating Pig Pen.

However, to my surprise, there came a time when I resented my writing being referred to as a hobby. Somewhere along the way

I began to see myself as a professional writer in spite of the kitchen table.

When you reach the point of looking at your writing as making a potentially serious contribution, however small, to Kingdom work, you have crossed an invisible line. Now it's time to look people in the eye when they ask what you do and say, "I am a writer." If you're like I was when I began, this seems to be a presumptuous statement, even after you begin racking up sales. But presumptuous or not, it is true. You *are* a writer.

To help you reach this conclusion, I suggest you develop a mission statement. Such a declaration of purpose keeps you focused on what you believe is your area of calling. It's easy to get sidetracked, but if you are not writing what you feel God has called you to do, then it's not writing on which you want to spend your time.

A mission statement can be as simple or complex as you choose. Mine is quite simple as is that of Jim Watkins who wrote chapter 11 of this book. My statement reads: "To write quality material that points to the fullness of life in Christ and to teach others to do/find the same." Jim's reads: "To communicate the Gospel of Christ in as effective and creative a manner as possible with as many people as possible." Both are brief and to the point.

However, another writer friend, Robin Jones Gunn of the *Christie Miller* and *Sierra Jensen* series as well as several romance novels in the *Palisades* line, has a longer, detailed statement. See the box on page 43.

Whether your statement is as succinct as Jim's and mine or as detailed as Robin's will probably be a function of your personality. It truly doesn't matter how simple or complex you choose to be. All that matters is that as a professional writer you can articulate a clear sense of God's purpose for your manuscripts.

Pray about what God wants you to be writing, understanding that He may call you to different types of writing at different times in your career. I know I have written different genres at different times, but my statement is general enough that I can write for children or adults, write fiction or nonfiction, teach or speak, and still be within the parameters of what I believe God has called me to.

However, because of my mission statement, I can filter out public relations writing, being secretary of every organization I'm

ROBIN'S MISSION STATEMENT FOR WRITING

GENERAL

Glorify God

1 Timothy 1:17: "Now to the King eternal, immortal, invisible, the only God, be honor and glory for ever and ever. Amen."

1 Corinthians 6:20: "You were bought at a price. Therefore honor God with your body."

Further His Kingdom

Matthew 6:10: "Your kingdom come, your will be done on earth as it is in heaven."

Be a Good Steward of the Gifts He's Given

Romans 11:29: "For God's gifts and his call are irrevocable."

1 Timothy 4:14: "Do not neglect your gift, which was given you."

SPECIFIC

Introduce Women to God, the Relentless Lover

Jeremiah 31:3: "I have loved you with an everlasting love; I have drawn you with loving-kindness."

Isaiah 43:1: "I have summoned you by name; you are mine."

Draw Others into an Authentic Relationship with Him through Biblical Truth

Romans 10:13-15: "Everyone who calls upon the name of the Lord will be saved. How, then, can they call on the one they have not believed in? And how can they believe in the one of whom they have not heard? And how can they hear without someone preaching to them? And how can they preach unless they are sent?"

Nudge Them Toward Faithful Obedience and Complete Surrender to God

1 Thessalonians 5:23: "May God himself, the God of peace, sanctify you through and through. May your whole spirit, soul and body be kept blameless at the coming of our Lord Jesus Christ."

involved in, spending time at colleges as an author in residence, or teaching junior high English (which I did pre-children). I can also turn down some speaking invitations with a clear conscience. Recently an editor friend approached me about setting up an editing service. I remembered my mission statement, which says I will write or teach, not edit. It was easy for me to thank him for the compliment and say a polite no.

You and the IRS

When you were a hobbyist writer, you declared any expenses for your writing on Schedule A of your tax forms. You were not allowed to declare any expenses beyond your income. If you had income beyond expenses, you declared that on Form 1040, "income for an activity not engaged in for profit." Now that you are a professional, things are different. Now you declare your income on Schedule C. Don't make the mistake of using the form that reads "Royalties." That form is for income from oil wells and such.

If you are still struggling with whether to call yourself a professional, the IRS suggests a number of factors that may help you reach a decision. As applied to writing, here's what to consider:

1. *The manner in which you conduct your writing:* How serious and professional are you in the conduct of your writing?
2. *The expertise of the taxpayer:* Have you the skills to actually write what you claim to be writing?
3. *The time and effort you spend on your writing:* Are you writing regularly, or is it a case of once a month if you're lucky?
4. *The expectation that the assets used in your writing will appreciate in value:* Do you expect to garner income from that article, or are you writing it merely (but no less importantly) for the comfort of friends?
5. *Your prior success in your writing:* Have you had responses to your writing as a hobbyist, or are you jumping right into a profession without any previous indication of your abilities?
6. *Your history of income or loss in your writing:* Have you had sales enough to indicate that you can operate in the black after a relatively short period of time?
7. *The amount of the profits:* Do your profits indicate you are seriously pursuing your writing? (Don't panic. We all, including the

IRS, know writers don't make much money. Still some profits ought to be discernible.)

8. *The taxpayer's overall finances*: Does your spouse's income provide enough to live on? For years I didn't make enough to keep a family of four off welfare; but in combination with my husband's income, we were solvent. Also, are you declaring yourself a professional writer for the purpose of a large tax write-off for that family trip you all took to Alaska? The IRS frowns on doing so.

9. *Elements of personal pleasure or recreation from your writing:* Do you write just for fun or for a purpose that is greater than recreation? Certainly those of us who write professionally derive pleasure from our occupation or we wouldn't be doing it; but there is more than pleasure involved. There's consistency, income, publication, and readers.

In a nutshell, in the eyes of the IRS, it basically comes down to the issue of profit motive. If a profit motive is missing, you have a hobby. If it's present, you have a profession.

"But I'm in ministry," you say. "I just want to serve the Lord."

Sure you do. So do we all. But we still have to pay the postage, buy the paper, and upgrade our computer systems regularly. Some of us even need to eat, pay the mortgage, send our kids to college, and finance our health insurance from our writing proceeds. The profit motive is plainly present no matter how spiritual we are.

One interesting aspect about being a writer is that frequently you will get income that the IRS has no way of knowing about. Perhaps a magazine pays you such a low sum that the IRS doesn't require them to report it. Perhaps as a writer you are asked to speak to a church group, and their honorarium also isn't reported to the IRS. The lack of reporting on the part of the payer isn't illegal if the payment is less than what the IRS requires. However, any lack of reporting on the part of the recipient of the money is illegal. As Christian writers, it is critical that we claim all our income. It's a matter of honesty and rendering unto Caesar that which is Caesar's.

YOU AND YOUR RECORDS

The surest way to impress the IRS with your professionalism is to keep excellent records.

By excellent records, I primarily mean receipts for *everything*: paper, pencils, pens, calendars (they keep track of your deadlines, writers' conferences, and speaking dates), mailers, postage, computers, printers, fax machines, telephone calls, stationery, file folders, books and magazines on writing, novels if you're a novelist, magazine subscriptions and books in your area of expertise, paper clips, scratch paper, business cards, pens, software, your online service, paint for your office, and writers' conference fees.

You should keep track of the mileage to your post office, your office supply store, your critique group, your writers' conference, your library, any speaking venue, as well as any research site. The mileage and date of every trip should be duly recorded since each mile is worth money at tax time, the exact amount set annually by the IRS.

When you declare yourself a professional, the IRS allows you to claim a loss two out of five years. It is the receipts that prove your loss is a valid claim. If you have to declare zero income other years, again the receipts are your validation.

Now that you are a professional, perhaps you want to claim a home office. You may do so provided: (1) The office is your primary place of business. If you have another office where you work a day job, don't claim a home office. (2) The office is used regularly and exclusively for your writing.

I have figured that my office is ten percent of our home. Since I use the room exclusively for writing, we can claim ten percent of all household expenses from heating to trash pickup to a new roof. Receipts from household expenses will provide me with the figure for my claim.

However, I must have a net profit before I can claim my home office. I can claim it to reduce my net profit to zero and carry any unclaimed loss forward into the next tax year. I cannot use it to claim a loss.

Conclusion

In some ways, regarding ourselves as professional writers is a matter of mind set. That's why we write our mission statements. That's why we tell people we are writers.

We recognize that professionalism requires certain ways of dealing with the IRS, and we understand that record keeping and creating a strong paper trail are imperative to verify any claims we make at tax time.

But as professional *Christian* writers, we acknowledge that the bottom line must always be: "Here, Lord, is a project that I have written. I offer it to You. Please do with it as You see fit. I ask that it sees print, that it touches lives, that it makes a difference in people. But because I am a committed Christian before I'm a professional writer, not my will but yours be done."

GAYLE G. ROPER has been a writer and speaker for more than twenty-five years and has had twenty-eight books published. She currently has a mystery series with Zondervan, which includes *Caught in the Middle* and *Caught in the Act*. She also has a Palisades romantic suspense series set in Bird-in-Hand, Pennsylvania, in the middle of Pennsylvania Dutch country. The titles include *The Key* and *The Document*. Gayle has also been published in many magazines, including *Discipleship Journal*, *Moody*, *The Lookout*, and *The Christian Communicator*. She not only speaks regularly at women's events but also teaches at writers' conferences across the country. She is also a member of the CLASSeminar staff. E-mail Gayle at: GGRoper@aol.com.

— 6 —

Writing Personal Experience Articles

KATHY COLLARD MILLER

For we cannot help speaking about
what we have seen and heard.
—ACTS 4:20

THE ABOVE VERSE CERTAINLY can be the theme of us who write personal experience articles or books because we have a passion to share what God has done in our lives and the lives of other people.

My writing career began with writing about a personal experience, the story of how God delivered me from being a child abuser. That article, which was the first article I ever sold, has been reprinted six times. I've also rewritten that story in other ways from different angles for five other articles. In addition, those stories have been reprinted numerous times. Of the one hundred plus articles I've sold, at least thirty-five have been personal experience stories, either my own or someone else's. Personal experience stories are an excellent genre because many magazines publish them.

INVESTIGATE POSSIBLE THEMES

Here are eight possible themes for personal experience stories.

Physical Healing/Coping

These stories focus on illness, death, handicaps, or injuries.

Emotional Healing/Coping

These stories deal with problems of fear, loneliness, widowhood, job loss, or addictions like alcohol, drugs, gambling, pornography.

Relationships

These experiences show how relationships were healed or improved or how acceptance of a poor relationship brought greater dependence on God.

Distant Past

A nostalgia piece deals with how someone changed, not just something cute that happened.

Adventure

Adventure stories feature people in dangerous or suspenseful situations.

Conversion

Testimony stories show how someone came to know the Lord, often focusing on the "before" of a lifestyle and that person's "present" relationship with God.

Personality Profile

A profile can be of a famous person or a person who has done something unique or important for the Lord. It may be written in as-told-to or with style. But it can also be written in third person.

For instance, I once wrote a personal experience story about a woman who overcame bulimia and then began a ministry to women suffering from eating disorders. I wrote this story in first person from her perspective, and the byline included her name and "as told to Kathy Collard Miller." The phrase *as told to* indicates the article was written by someone else in the first person mode.

Organization/Ministry/Service

This story tells about the efforts of a group which is serving the Lord in some way or an individual who is ministering for God in personal ministry.

With an organization, it's usually a good idea to tell the story through the eyes of one person involved because it makes it more personal and interesting. That person may be the founder, president, someone benefiting from their services, or a volunteer working with them. Even though you are reporting a story, you will want to use fiction techniques so it won't sound like you are. It may be appropriate to make a composite "person" of many people involved if there needs to be anonymity or privacy.

Look again at this list of the eight types of personal experience stories. Which ones could you immediately begin to write about?

INTERVIEW FOR INFORMATION

If you are going to write someone else's story, you'll need to interview that person for the information. At times, you may even have the opportunity to interview a celebrity or well-known person. If you have someone you want to interview, there are two ways to proceed: Obtain permission from the interviewee, or generate the interest of the editor. If the interviewee is reluctant to be covered in an article, you may be able to override that reluctance by saying you have an editor interested in the story.

In preparation for your interview, read everything about that person and articles and books he or she has written. If you are interviewing someone who has not been published, you could submit questions before the interview to get basic information. That way you will not go into the interview without some knowledge of who you are interviewing.

Let this information inspire you to write down interview questions. Then group questions in categories for your interview notes.

During your interview, start with the simplest questions. These will most likely be the easiest to answer, and you'll put the person at ease. I once made the mistake in an interview of making my first questions deep and theological. The interviewee was taken aback, and I could tell she felt uncomfortable. She may have felt like I was attacking her; but, of course, that was not my intention.

During the interview, tape the conversation and take notes. It may seem redundant to do both. But there is nothing more horrifying then returning from an interview, turning on the tape recorder, and finding nothing there. As you take notes, double space your writing, so that there will be space for transcribing your notes later.

Once you've interviewed your subject and begin writing the personal experience story, keep in mind the following ideas for writing in a powerful way.

SHOW—DON'T TELL

Telling uses passive verbs like *be* and *was*. Showing uses powerful verbs. The concept of showing is especially important in writing personal experience stories because it's through showing that the reader will become involved and touched at an emotional level.

Here are some examples. Instead of writing "I was afraid," write: "My throat felt dry and I couldn't swallow. *What am I doing here?* I wondered, as I rubbed my sweat-soaked hands on my jeans." Instead of writing "She was uncomfortable," write: "She wiggled in her chair as if she were sitting on an anthill. Her eyes darted back and forth between me and the minister."

Can you see the difference? Telling is passive and boring. But when we show, we powerfully communicate through the senses.

USE DIALOGUE FREQUENTLY

Show an individual's personality and the choices he or she makes through interaction with others. Obviously, doing so takes more words and space on a page; and in a limited-word article, it could be a problem. But you can still use this technique as much as possible.

For instance, in an article entitled "My Mother Has Alzheimer's," the author, Sharon Fish, effectively uses dialogue to describe the condition of her mother:

I can still remember that day in the doctor's office when Mom was diagnosed. Her conversation with the young neurology resident served to reinforce their findings:

"I just want to ask you a few questions, Mrs. Fish," he began.

"Okay," my mother replied.

"What year is it?" he asked.

"It's 1960," she said.

"No, its 1980," he corrected. "What month is it?"

"May," she answered.

"No, it's December. What's today's date?"

"The first. Is that right?"

"No, it's the tenth. What is the day of the week?"

"You're so smart, you tell me," my mother said.[2]

Sharon effectively used dialogue to communicate her mother's condition. She could have written, "It was sad when my mother was diagnosed with Alzheimer's by a young neurology doctor." That statement lacks the power that was communicated through the dialogue between the doctor and Sharon's mother.

SHOW ACTION AND/OR EMOTION

If a person is angry, show her throwing something or yelling. If he is feeling depressed, show him staring at the TV by the hour. Use strong emotional words like *furious*, *despairing*, *jubilant*, or *brokenhearted*. For example, I wanted to do that in my personal experience story entitled, "Child Abuse: I Was a Part of the Epidemic." Here are the opening paragraphs of that article.

> I rounded the corner of our living room and stopped. My two-year-old daughter, Sandy, sat on the edge of the fireplace sifting ashes through her fingers. The black cinders littered the carpet and bricks.
>
> "Sandy!" I yelled. "I've told you three times today...don't play in the fireplace!"
>
> Anger boiled within me. I didn't need another mess to clean up with company coming that evening. I strode over to her, yanked her up by her arm, and began hitting her bottom and legs. "Look at the mess you've made," I shrieked as my hand slapped against her skin again and again. "Why do you keep disobeying me?"
>
> Sandy's hysterical screaming finally brought me back to reason. I sank to the floor beside her and cradled my head in my hands. "Oh God," I pleaded, "I did it again! I promised I would control myself today. What happened?"[1]

Writing with emotions and action makes the reader want to continue reading.

Keep Instruction Subtle

Don't refer directly to the reader using the word *you*. If you do, it will come across as preachy and turn the reader off. Also it can destroy the atmosphere of having the reader feel that he or she is a part of the story.

I struggled with that concept early in my writing. The first book idea I had was to instruct parents on how to deal with their frustration. But the editors I contacted said that I was not qualified to give such instruction. Instead, they suggested I write my personal experience in story form. I resisted that idea because I wanted to give practical ideas that would help people. When I finally gave up, I wrote my personal experience book now called *Help for Hurting Moms;* and I've found that parents have been helped as they read it. They experience and learn from what I went through. Teaching is included without it being technically direct instruction because the readers learn through example.

If you're fearful that your strong message isn't going to get across without preaching to the readers, remember the Holy Spirit teaches people, using your written words.

If both you and your editor believe practical instruction is necessary, an option to consider is the sidebar. A sidebar is information encased in a border, separate from the article. It can be a useful way to communicate further information or suggestions for change.

Avoid Using Every Detail

Details may have had significance for you; but unless they're truly significant to the story, omit them. A good idea is to get the input of an objective reader, a critique group, or an editorial service.

Also don't get distracted onto "rabbit trails." Rabbit-trail writing goes off in a different direction than the purpose of the article. Keep to your point. Have only one main theme or focus.

Help the Reader See

Give short, concise descriptions of the surroundings. Describe clothing, appearance, facial expressions, or other facts that will help the reader's mental eye. For an article, these must be short but powerful, including what's really important. For a book, you can go into more detail.

DIVE RIGHT IN

Sometimes the hardest thing to do is start the story. It is best not to give a great deal of background at first. Dive right into your story and the people involved. When I am first working on a personal experience story, or any article for that matter, I usually end up cutting the opening two paragraphs of the first draft. It seems like I am cutting information the reader should know, but usually the story is fine without it. If not, I can work it in later.

For example, here's a first draft for my personal experience story about being an angry mother.

> I didn't know how I'd become so angry after becoming a mother, but just gradually I'd become a screaming meamie. All day long it seemed like I couldn't say a positive thing to my two-year-old daughter. Why was I acting like this?
>
> One day I found Darcy playing in the fireplace for the third time that day and I screamed, "Darcy, how many times do I have to tell you? Don't play in the fireplace."

I edited these paragraphs to the following sentence: " I marched over to two-year-old Darcy and screamed, 'Darcy, how many times do I have to tell you? Don't play in the fireplace.'"

Get right into the story. If things need to be explained, do that after your introduction. You want to grab the reader's attention quickly.

BE CAUTIOUS

There should be a certain amount of emotional healing before telling any story about those who have experienced trauma or victimization. Total healing isn't necessary or possible in most cases, but there must be a certain amount of objectivity in order for you to be able to share your story without other issues clouding the purpose and message. For instance, if you are a victim in the story and you haven't forgiven the perpetrator, bitterness and resentment may come across.

It's all right to identify and admit where healing still needs to occur. You could say: "Although I'm not totally healed yet from this experience, I have seen the Lord work on some issues in my life; and I'm confident He'll continue to do that."

Another caution is to understand that you don't have to give a happy ending if it's not true. "They lived happily ever after" stories can sometimes be a disservice because readers wonder why their lives aren't working out the same way. Be real and honest about any continuing struggles or weaknesses if they are pertinent to the story.

After you've finished writing another person's story, send a copy of it for the subject's approval. Although not everyone does so, I find this step is not only courteous but also helps to make my work more accurate. I may have misunderstood something the person said, and he or she will be able to correct it.

Once you have written your personal experience story, refer to the *Christian Writers' Market Guide* for magazines, take-home papers, or book publishers who publish personal experience stories.

I trust that after your story is published, you'll receive letters like I have, thanking you for sharing your experience. God has used my writing to encourage Christians in their walk with God and unbelievers to come to know Him in a personal way. Some time ago, I received a letter from a woman in Sultanate of Oman, saying she had received Christ as a result of reading what I wrote. That was a thrill! And I know the Lord will use your personal experience stories in the same way.

ENDNOTES

1. Kathy Collard Miller, "Child Abuse: I Was a Part of the Epidemic," *Psychology for Living* (May 1984).
2. Sharon Fish, "My Mother Has Alzheimer's," *Today's Christian Woman* (September/October 1990), p. 8.

KATHY COLLARD MILLER is the author of over thirty-five books, including the best-selling *God's Vitamin "C" for the Spirit* and *God's Abundance*. She is also the author of the audio tape series and workbooks for *Writing Professionally and Speaking Professionally*. She speaks fifty times a year across our nation and internationally on spiritual growth and relationships. Contact her at P.O. Box 1058, Placentia, CA 92871; phone: 714 993-2654; or e-mail: Kathyspeak@aol.com.

— 7 —

Using the Internet for Research

STEVEN R. LAUBE

However great a man's natural talent may be, the act of writing cannot be learned all at once.

—JEAN JACQUES ROUSSEAU

IMAGINE HAVING A PERSONAL library the size of Manhattan available 24 hours a day, 365 days a year at your fingertips. Virtually any question could be answered with a little research. But imagine that same library without a card catalog or central organization. Everything in the place is packed in different boxes set around the building at random. The joy of having that information available is quickly destroyed by the incredible frustration experienced trying to find it.

Welcome to the Internet—one of the greatest repositories of human knowledge ever compiled. But it is also one of the most disorganized masses of information ever compiled. Among the marvelous gems are reams of useless junk. It can be compared to a massive flea market. If you have the patience, you can find some real treasures. But few of us have the time, energy, or patience to sift through the mounds of stuff just to find a nugget of worth. Prabhakar Raghavan, a top-rated IBM computer scientist, recently said, "I'm constantly amazed at the extremely arcane information on the Web."

Most people have taken the Internet for a spin and have become discouraged by the sheer mass of useless information they have to wade through. Discouraged and frustrated, they give up with a vow to avoid the Internet altogether.

Don't despair! There are a few simple techniques that can make your Web surfing a pleasure.[1] In this chapter I assume a small measure of prior computer and Internet experience, because there is not enough space to create a full tutorial on the use of the Worldwide Web.

Successful Searches

While editing a book on rock music for Bethany House Publishers, the author decided we needed to create a list of Christian rock music organized by genre (rock, rap, alternative, contemporary, gospel, etc.). After a short discussion, because of time constraints, my boss felt I should be the one to create the list. Unfortunately, after being out of the Christian retailing business for many years, my knowledge of Christian bands was somewhat limited.

First I went to a Christian bookstore. While it was helpful to get a grasp of the number of groups, the music was organized alphabetically by artist, not by genre. The album covers gave some hints but not enough information to go on. So I went on the Internet and searched for contemporary Christian music. This search resulted in a number of Web sites created by fans who listed their favorite bands by genre. I compiled their opinions and results into one large document and ran the list by teenagers and a youth worker. That list is now part of the book. Time spent on the Internet: two hours.

Another Bethany House author was researching a book on Roman Catholicism. He came across a quote attributed to the Pope in the late 1800s. However, this quote was from a secondary source. Was it quoted accurately? What was the context in which it was spoken? How could he find the original source?

He could travel to a major Catholic university, or go to the Vatican. Or he could go on the Internet. There he found a Web site that had all the words spoken or written by every Pope as far back in history as possible. The author went to the year in which that quote was purportedly spoken. He copied each page of information from that year and pasted the text into one large document. Then he used the find function of his word processor.

In seconds the computer found the quote, intact, and in context. The results of that search is now an accurate primary resource footnote in the finished book. Time spent on the Internet: one hour.

SEARCH ENGINES

The above examples show that search engines are the key to successful research on the Internet. These are computer programs that have been designed to hunt for information in a pool of data called a database. They act like a full blown set of white and yellow pages for the data on the Internet.

Search engines find their information through keywords provided by the user. When you ask a search engine to find something using a particular keyword, it sifts through its entire database of Web sites to find it and present you a list of matching references, or hits.

Most first-time users of a search engine are overwhelmed by the number of hits they receive for a keyword. For instance, type in the keywords *sports injuries*, and you can receive up to 1.7 million hits! It would take weeks to visit and read all the information pulled by that one simple inquiry.

So what do you do? Below I will take you through many of the major search engines to give you some tips on how to maximize their use. Be aware that the Internet is always in a state of flux. While my analysis is as current as possible, these search engine companies constantly are improving their software interfaces. Try each engine yourself to determine which one will serve your needs the best.

Search engine Web sites generate their income from selling advertisements that appear on their pages. Be prepared to be confronted with a new ad on every page during your search. Some search engines even have the ability to show you an ad that is related to the search you just conducted. Don't be surprised to see an ad for a hotel and resort if you ask for information about Hawaii.

For best results, use quotes around the words in your search query. For example, type "used pianos" instead of just the word *piano*. Doing so will find all Web pages that have both *used* and *pianos* in their indexes.

AltaVista™ (www.altavista.digital.com)

AltaVista™ has been called the original plain-vanilla search engine. It has the largest database on the Web with over 140 million Web pages consisting of 200 gigabytes of information.

While boasting it is the largest database, AltaVista™ usually generates an excess number of unrelated hits, some of which are broken links that go nowhere. It works well as an alternative search engine, but should not be your primary starting point.

Excite (www.excite.com)

Encompassing over 55 million Web pages, Excite is a dynamic and highly usable search engine. Excite has partnered with a number of other companies to become the underlying search engine program. (See America Online's AOL Find as an example.)

My current computer came pre-installed with Microsoft's Internet Explorer 4.0. On the toolbar along the top is a button called "search." When selected, this button opens a new window that is a shortcut to the Excite search engine. If you know where to look, you can change this default setting; but I prefer to leave it alone.

The best part of the Excite search engine is their Search Wizard. After the initial search, the engine dynamically creates a list of the top ten words that help you refine the context of your search. These words are generated by a gigantic index where words are clustered into related groups. Your hits are ranked by percentage of accuracy. In most cases you can find the information you need in the top forty hits.

Excite also offers a free e-mail service and a home page for each user that can be personalized to his or her specific interests. See http://my.excite.com.

This search engine is a must-use resource for any Internet researcher.

Infoseek (www.infoseek.com)

Similar in look and feel to Excite, Infoseek pulls its data from an index of 30 million pages. You also have the option of searching Internet newsgroups, news, or business information in addition to the traditional Web sites.

Be prepared to be overwhelmed by the number of hits you receive. The next step is to search just the list of hits by entering new, more refined keywords and select "Search within results." The advanced search option will allow you to search just within a particular Web site. For example, you could search for all information regarding Microsoft Word 97 within the www.microsoft.com Web site.

Recently Infoseek formed a partnership with the Disney Corporation with the goal of completely rehauling its engine and information. Look for significant improvements of an already unique and helpful search site.

Lycos (www.lycos.com)

With an index of 30 million pages, Lycos is the same size as Infoseek, but Lycos' greatest strength is its ability to search for sound and images. Hits created are links to graphics on Web pages stored in Lycos' database. You can't see them until you click on them, but its search for multimedia is the fastest of all the search engines.

Another impressive feature is the natural language query. You can type your search in the form of a question, such as, "Who are the winners of the Nobel Prize for Literature?" The results of these queries can be quite astounding.

Lycos also has a filtering program called SafteyNet that prevents searches on offensive and pornographic words. Hits containing vile adult content are forced to the end of the search results page where they are likely not to be found. Users must register before using the feature, but it is a wonderful addition for those of us who wish to avoid being confronted by detestable material.

With its smaller database, Lycos has a hard time beating Excite for sheer information; but its SafteyNet and natural language query features make this a great choice for any researcher.

Yahoo! (www.Yahoo.com)

Yahoo! is the granddaddy of all search engines. While it does not have the largest database by any means (reports vary as to its actual size), it is the only search engine that is indexed by hand instead of by machine. This fact means that nearly every hit generated has been created by the indexing efforts of a human database engineer, a process that may reduce the number of hits but creates a much higher quality.

Instead of returning results by percentage or keyword, Yahoo! organizes the list by topics or categories. Yahoo! has a master index of 25,000 different categories under which all the Web sites are organized. This process significantly increases the likelihood of finding the information you are looking for. Imagine my gratification on entering the keywords "Christian self-publishing" and have ACW Press, my self-publishing company, listed first!

A hidden feature of Microsoft's Internet Explorer 4.0 web browser is the ability to search the Yahoo! site without having to first visit its start page. In the box where you usually enter a Web address (i.e., www.christiancommunicator.com), type a question mark and then your keywords inside quotation marks (? "honda accord"). This query takes you immediately to a page on Yahoo! that lists the results of your search.

Like Excite, Yahoo! also provides a free e-mail service and a personalized home page. I use Yahoo! as my personal home page that opens when I start Internet Explorer for the first time. On that page I receive up-to-the-minute news, stock reports, sports scores, weather, and news clippings about publishing. For those who do not use America Online or CompuServe, this is a quick and easy way to stay in touch with current information. (See http://my.yahoo.com.)

I prefer to use Yahoo! as my first search engine option. The category designations help narrow down the number of hits received and increase the chance to find what I'm looking for quickly. However, the size of the Yahoo! database is somewhat limiting when looking for obscure information.

MetaCrawler (www.metacrawler.com)

MetaCrawler is a megasearch engine that accesses multiple search engines all at the same time. Rather than maintaining a database of its own, MetaCrawler does a cross section search of AltaVista™, Yahoo!, Excite, Infoseek, WebCrawler (not mentioned above), and Lycos.

Type in your key words and then choose the button "any" which means that any of the supplied words will be present in the search results. Choosing "all" means that all the keywords must be present in the results. Choosing "as a phrase" means that the exact phrase, in the order it is typed, must be present in the results.

The results are listed in order of relevance given to the search criteria by the other search engines. Hits are ranked from a high of 1,000 to a low of 1. Included in the search results are the names of the search engines that have this information, which helps determine the quality of the hit.

The drawback of this engine is the reliance on the MetaCrawler software to properly rank the hits by relevance. While usually very helpful, there are occasions where the results are confusing. While I use Yahoo! as my first choice and Excite as my second, MetaCrawler is fast becoming a more common place to go for information.

Using the Internet is not like going to the public library and looking among the stacks until you find the relevant section. The library is methodically organized along the Dewey Decimal system or the Library of Congress Catalog numbering system. The Internet is much different. It is more like an eccentric man who likes to collect things but never likes to organize them.

Search engines are an indispensable tool for Internet research. The key to good results is first to use quotation marks around your keywords. Secondly, think hard about the specific nature of your search. If you are just casually browsing, you can be overwhelmed by the results. But if you plan your search, you will be much happier with the outcome.

ENDNOTE

1. I have created a Web site that is specifically designed for the writer. There you will find links to over 100 other pages, organized by topic. I have included links to all the search engines mentioned in this chapter. Go to http://www.acwpress.com/links.htm.

STEVEN R. LAUBE is the senior editor of non-fiction books for Bethany House Publishers and the executive editor of ACW Press. A veteran of nearly twenty years in the publishing industry, he began in the Christian bookstore business. The store he managed was named the National Store of the Year by the Christian Booksellers Association out of 4,000 eligible stores in 1989. He served as the national buyer for a large bookstore chain. In addition, he has worked as the manager of information services for the Evangelical Christian Publishers Association. He is the author of *God's Promises for Your Financial Success* and has edited nearly 100 books. He is married and has three children.

— 8 —

Writing Daily Devotionals

MARY LOU REDDING

The good writers touch life often.
—RAY BRADBURY

WRITERS OF DAILY DEVOTIONALS—and in fact all Christian writers—face a special challenge. We write about relationship with a God who is invisible, intangible, and unlimited. Yet, we do so for creatures who are corporeal, limited, and sensory in their approach to the world. We write to deepen relationship with our God who lovingly and unrelentingly seeks us all, but we write for humans who are capricious and inconsistent in attending to God's call. Such a task is both a great privilege and a great responsibility.

We have only moments of our readers' attention; yet those moments can affect eternal relationships. So we must use well every tool and technique available to us as we seek to help others deepen their devotion and responsiveness to God.

Writing short devotionals requires careful attention to craft. Since relatively few words convey our message, each one must carry maximum impact. Devotionals may appear to be easy to write, but that is only appearance. Writing short pieces well is a challenge for all writers, including experienced ones.

I'm reminded of a story I read about Abraham Lincoln. Someone asked him to speak to a group, and he asked how much time he would have. When asked why that was important, he said something like, "If I can speak for two hours, I won't need to prepare. If I can speak for only twenty minutes, that will require some preparation. But if I will have only two minutes, that will require a great deal of preparation." In other words, the fewer words we have, the harder we must work to distill our message.

Characteristics of Good Devotions

Good devotional writing has eight characteristics that we can incorporate into writing of many kinds.

Scriptural Base

Good devotional writing is grounded firmly in Scripture study and meditation on its meaning for our lives. We cannot pour from an empty pitcher, so those who wish to write quality devotionals must spend time with the Bible. As we do so, to quote Lord Chesterfield's advice, we will find that our writing has "a power above its own." Some of the power and wisdom of the Bible will be interwoven with our words.

Integration

Good devotional writing is not merely a cute or touching story with a Bible verse tacked on. Though some writers find or compose a story and then use a concordance to find a verse to use with it, the most effective and powerful meditations grow more organically from Scripture. They integrate Scripture's content in such a way that the Scripture and the meditation cannot be separated from one another. Readers will sense not only that the Scripture "fits" but that no other passage could be used.

When we read and study the Bible, Scripture will be used responsibly because it will reflect the larger context. At *The Upper Room* we once received a meditation that used the story of King David and Shimei as the basis for a devotional about mercy and forgiveness. Shimei was an enemy of King David. Rather than executing Shimei, however, David placed him under house arrest. David told Shimei if he stayed inside the compound, he would not be harmed; but if he came outside, he would be killed. The writer used this event as an example of mercy and forgiveness. The Bible tells us, however, that Shimei eventually left the compound. When he did, David kept his word and had Shimei killed. The overall context of this story is not mercy and forgiveness. The writer chose to use only a part of the passage without stepping back to see the incident in its larger context. In strong meditations, Scripture is used responsibly in its entire context, with the writer's personal story woven into the Scripture's message.

Authenticity

Good devotional writing is authentic. It sounds like a real person writing to other real people about what it means to live faithfully in a particular situation. In the Middle Ages, theologians carried on a discussion trying to settle the question of how many angels could dance on the head of a pin. Though such discussions may be fascinating to some, they have little to do with people's actual struggles. Good meditations deal not with how many angels can dance anywhere but with what people face in daily life—questions about relationships with God and people. Authentic meditations acknowledge that life is complex and sometimes difficult, while pointing to hope in God.

Such writing is not falsely sweet, tying up every dilemma neatly with a bow on top. Preaching has been described as "filling twenty minutes with holy sound." Some writers seem to think meditations are the written equivalent of this—pretty language presented in familiar and comforting cadences.

Substance

Good devotional writing is not merely pleasant-sounding words that make people feel good. Rather, it can stir people to examine themselves and move beyond their comfort zones to consider new ideas and new ways of serving God. As someone has said, "God comes not only to comfort the afflicted but to afflict the comfortable." Good devotional writing allows people to enter into the experiences of others, to walk with other pilgrims who are trying to be faithful to God's call, and as they do so to see the world in new ways.

Real people know they are imperfect. Perfect people in perfect families, finding neat solutions to their problems, are difficult for readers to identify with. Good meditations show people as they really are in daily life, while showing that God's grace is available and active in those daily situations.

Worthwhile Message

Good devotional writing is a fair trade. The reader trades time, effort, and attention for what the writer has to say. If a reader feels that the message or insight is worth the effort expended in reading, that is a fair trade. A writer who gives readers grief—who writes prose that is difficult slogging—will lose readers.

Readers need to be gathering information and insight, not sharpening their reading skills. Sometimes writers may be tempted to exercise all their stylistic muscles, to demonstrate their mastery of vocabulary and complex sentence structure. Readers don't care about our vocabulary and mastery of compound, complex sentences. They care about what will help them. If we write long sentences using complex vocabulary and convey only a small grain of insight or help, most readers will not consider that a fair trade. Devotional writing should not be a test of reading skill. It should be accessible to readers.

One way of thinking about this characteristic is to consider how people feel about poetry. Most people don't read it often. Why? Because understanding and enjoying poetry requires more mental effort than reading prose.

Adults learn on the basis of perceived need; when they feel a need to find out about something, they look for information. When they feel a need to know God, they seek information about how to know God. Their goal is information, not literary growth or mental challenge. This means that writing that draws attention to itself because of its use of rhyme, rhythm, alliteration, or cleverly turned phrases may actually be evidence that the writer has failed.

As Christian writers, we want to direct our readers' attention to God and God's truth. If readers say, "My, isn't that beautifully written," or "That person really knows how to turn a phrase," we have directed their attention not to God but to us. Our writing should be almost invisible; it should not draw attention to itself. Strunk and White's book *The Elements of Style* offers help in writing more concisely, clearly, and directly.

Concreteness and Sensory Appeal

Good devotional writing is concrete and sensory. It invites readers into the author's experience or exploration through the use of words and images that engage the reader's senses—hearing, sight, taste, touch, smell. Writers must build a bridge from their ideas and insights to the reader's experiences and emotions.

We do so by using words that paint pictures, that sing songs, that dance, that carry aromas to our readers' noses. We invite readers not only to read our ideas but to interact with them on other levels as well. We do this by getting readers to open their own treasure chests of sensory memories. We write about God's truth, but we do so using images that call forth readers' sensory associations. 1 John 1:1 says, "Which we have seen with our eyes, which...our hands have touched." Though the stuff of daily lives may seem too mundane to write about, familiar images have power to evoke strong responses in our readers.

Consider the images Jesus used to help His readers understand Him and the role He wanted to have in their lives. Jesus did not talk about being the Incarnation. He did not use words like redemption, atonement, or even theology. He called himself the Bread, the Door, the Path, the Light, and the Good Shepherd.

When Jesus called himself the Bread of Life, He was speaking to people who smelled bread baking every day as they walked through their villages. They knew how their mouths watered when they were hungry. Jesus conveyed much more than a theological idea in that phrase. He hooked into His listeners' sensory memories. When He called himself the Living Water, He was talking to people who lived near a desert. Water was life; to be without it was to die.

Jesus invited people to consider eternal truths by linking them to common activities, by weaving them into stories about sons and daughters, sheep and goats, bread and yeast. We want to write about doorknobs, light switches, or morning traffic in such a way that when our readers next encounter these things, they will be reminded of some spiritual truth.

Having said all this about including images, it is also important not to overdo them. Writers sometimes load in so many images or sensory associations that readers cannot sort them—and they should not have to.

Most meditations should confine themselves to one dominant image, more like a single snapshot than a photo album. Several years ago, we published a meditation about a woman floating in a large inner tube on a sun-dotted lake, dangling her hands as she floated. She wrote about the warmth of the sun and the water, comparing them to what it feels like to be supported by God's love. This single image takes a theological abstraction, being supported by God's love, and links it with a tactile experience. Anyone who has ever taken a warm bath can make associations with her experience and, from there, perhaps understand how it feels to trust God and rest in His care. Even now, years later, I remember the spiritual point she made. When we write in this way, we increase the staying power of the insights we seek to convey.

Universality

Good devotional writing is universal in two senses. First, for a magazine like *The Upper Room* that circulates in many countries and languages, material must transcend cultures. Many daily devotional magazines that circulate only in English and primarily in the United States are able to use material that we must return.

Some subjects—dating to choose a spouse, dieting, or medical technology—are difficult to use in cultures other than our own. Dating is a Western phenomenon. In many places, marriages are arranged; and unmarried men and women are never alone together until they are officially engaged. Dieting and preoccupation with weight are peculiarly Western. In most places in the world, the issue is not eating too much but getting enough to eat. Though a meditation about dieting as a spiritual issue might appeal to many in this country, it would not be helpful in Africa or Asia. Medical technology that we are familiar with and take for granted in this country is often unavailable elsewhere and presents problems for translators and readers in other places.

All daily devotional magazines screen material according to their individual criteria. The screens are different, but all editorial processes have them. Therefore, material that is not accepted by one magazine may be usable by another.

Secondly, good meditations are universal in that they help readers make the link between the writer's particular experience and a general truth that others can apply in their lives. In the meditation I mentioned earlier, after writing about the experience of floating on the lake, the writer said, "Whenever I'm tired, worried, hurt, or depressed, I close my eyes, relax, and imagine myself back at the lake, floating in the 'warm streak.' But it's not water I'm floating in. Instead, I am immersed in God's warm and healing love."

Everyone has times of feeling tired, worried, hurt, or depressed; and this writer offers a strategy for entering into God's healing presence during those times. She moves from her particular experience to universal situations with which we all can identify. This kind of writing invites readers to linger in God's presence, to enrich their meditating on God's goodness.

Encouragement to See God

Writing meditations offers training in paying attention to what God is doing around us all the time. Those who write devotionals form the habit of looking for God's activity in the midst of daily life, and those who look will find that they see God more and more.

BENEFITS FOR WRITERS

Writing short meditations has several benefits for writers. Beginning writers may find daily devotional magazines a good place to make their first sales. When an editor decides to publish a writer's work, that editor decides to commit the publication's resources to that writer. Publishing a meditation or a short article by an unknown writer represents a small risk—much smaller than the risk a publisher takes with a book, for instance—and editors are willing to take small risks.

Also, writing short meditations is an opportunity to polish writing skills and reinforce a commitment to continually be sending material to publishers. The training in striving to write clearly and concisely, use strong images, and make every word count can transfer to weightier projects.

Writers who work for months or even years on huge projects may need small successes to encourage them along the way, and devotionals are projects that writers can complete and submit in a relatively short time.

A meditation is short enough that writers can use it to work on refining their craft even if they have only small blocks of time to give to writing. Completing a project is energizing, and writers immersed in huge projects may need the encouragement of finishing and submitting smaller pieces, such as devotionals.

Source for Ideas

Daily life offers a continually growing and renewed source of illustrations and ideas, a staple every writer needs. And while we are gathering these, we also deepen our sense of God's partnership with us—which brings us back to where I began: Good devotional writing grows out of our personal spiritual lives. This is both the fountain from which we drink and the well from which we draw to refresh and strengthen others.

Mary Lou Redding is managing editor of *The Upper Room* magazine, an international, interdenominational, daily devotional guide. *The Upper Room* is published in sixty-three editions and forty-three languages and circulates in more than eighty countries. Mary Lou teaches frequently at writers' conferences in the United States and abroad. She is an award-winning writer. Her first book, *Breaking and Mending: Divorce and God's Grace*, was published in 1998. She serves on the editorial advisory boards of *Horizons*, a magazine published by UPCUSA, and *Pockets* magazine for children, published by The Upper Room. She is the mother of an adult daughter.

— 9 —

A Different Kind of Mission Field: Writing for the Secular Market

KAREN O'CONNOR

As long as it is day, we must do the work of him who sent me. Night is coming, when no one can work."

—JOHN 9:4

SOME CHRISTIAN WRITERS VIEW the secular market as they do the mission fields of Africa. They don't want to go there! It is easier and safer to write for believers, to build a writing ministry this side of the Great Divide—that invisible line that separates spiritual from secular.

But if we are to take seriously God's command to share Christ's love with all nations, then we must look with more than a passing glance at writing for the "nations" of the secular market. People everywhere are thirsty for the Living Water, Jesus—even if they don't know it.

We can quench that thirst by writing about topics that reflect and reveal God's love while at the same time honor the boundaries established by the publisher. I have done this successfully for nearly twenty-five years, and it has been a very satisfying part of my writing life—in addition to writing books and articles for the Christian market.

One of the easiest and most productive ways to penetrate this ground is to write how-to articles. People everywhere are looking for help: how to lead a more meaningful life, how to parent their children, how to get along with coworkers, and everything in between. As assignments and sales multiply, your byline will reach increasing numbers of readers; and you will build a name for yourself. Your reputation will be built on quality work, timely submissions, cooperative relations, and respectful treatment of readers and editors. These characteristics alone speak volumes about the kind of person you are. Living and writing with integrity is always noticed.

All of the above may accumulate without so much as the mention of God's name. But no matter. You will be spreading the Lord's love and compassion by your presence in print, by your choice of topics, by the words you use, and by the tone in which you express yourself. And if you and I don't write these articles, someone else will—someone who doesn't know the Lord as we do.

I have had people come up to me after speaking engagements, and I've received notes following their reading of articles or books of mine, asking me about my spiritual life. They noticed something different about me. "What is it?" people want to know.

That question leads to an opportunity to share the truth from my experience. One woman actually turned herself in to the police for embezzling funds from her employer after she read my book *When Spending Takes the Place of Feeling* (written for both Christian and secular readers). She came back to Christ as a result of what I wrote! Such power to influence is humbling. And we all have it—by the authority and grace of the Holy Spirit.

A man in his eighties who had been estranged from his extended family told me—after reading my article in *Reader's Digest* on the importance of "being there" for people—that he was overcome by the awareness of his selfishness. He said he put down the article, went to the phone immediately, and called his brother to apologize and accept an invitation to a family reunion. Imagine the healing that occurred all because of my conviction to write an article for a secular magazine on a subject of spiritual significance. These opportunities abound in each of our lives if we remain open to them and then act on them.

Sources for writing for the secular market are at hand—just as they are when writing for the Christian market. The following steps will lead you to that well of ideas right there in your own backyard.

DRAW FROM YOUR LIFE EXPERIENCES

Consider your background, education, and hobbies for easy-to-access material. If you're a teacher or parent, you probably have suggestions for students and other parents. "Study Less but Learn More," "How to Make Better Use of Your Time," and "How to Earn Your Summer Fun" are a few of the titles I've sold easily. Each one of these topics lends itself to suggestions that open the reader to such spiritual truths as kindness, patience, love, and compassion.

For example, I encouraged kids to make better use of their time (other than watching TV or talking on the phone) by running errands for the elderly or ill, helping neighborhood parents by playing with their children, preparing a surprise meal for someone in need, organizing a junior Olympics or a backyard craft fair on their block, or collecting books for a homeless shelter.

If knitting, woodworking, camping, surfing, or animal training is part of your experience, share that corner of your world with readers of specialty magazines. "Puppy Health—Tips from a Dog's Best Friend" came quickly after my family reared a batch of Boston Terriers one summer. I sold it immediately to a dog fanciers' magazine. I included anecdotes from our family's experience, thereby sharing the reverence for life that is a priority in our family—even when it comes to dogs!

"How to Communicate with Your Baby" sold to a confession magazine of all places. I saw it as another opportunity to plant a seed of love and encouragement in mothers who may desperately need it.

DO YOUR RESEARCH

What you don't live through you can look up, or add to your experience by reading what others have done. Then turn these facts and figures into creative nonfiction. Careful research can yield a harvest of articles from one source. For example, I produced the following articles for parents of preschoolers: "Your Child's First Friends," "Parents—A Child's First Teachers," "Learning Games—Fun for Parents and Preschoolers," and "How Does Your Child See Himself?" (on self-image). Each of these articles gave me opportunities to share my Christian values in a positive, yet subtle way.

I did a mountain of research on ecology and conservation for articles and a book for children. The result was a combination of information and self-help. Later I used this same research for a fiction series I wrote for young readers on God's green earth. My writing reflected my reverence for God's creation; His resources such as water, wood, plants, and animals; and our duty and privilege to take care of them. I didn't preach a sermon. I simply revealed the facts through real-life anecdotes and ended with suggestions for how each one of us can do something every day to preserve the natural gifts we've been given. That way there is plenty for everyone to use and enjoy.

Tap Other People's Expertise

When interviewing experts for my articles, I choose people I respect and can count on to give me information that will uphold my point of view as a Christian. For example, I interviewed a school librarian for an article I wrote on how to bring kids and books together. Without any prompting on my part, Mrs. Bronsen offered the following advice: "Reading not only stimulates self-confidence in children but also helps them achieve a spiritual awareness, especially through fiction. Somehow good books help children see the difference between good and evil, right and wrong. And we have the opportunity for genuine family happenings through books."

"How About Becoming a Foot Doctor?" and "How to Care for Baby's Feet" sold to *Young Miss* and *Baby Talk*, both secular magazines that rely on the advice of experts to support the author's perspective. I had the privilege of interviewing a respected podiatrist for both articles. He did not offer any specifically spiritual advice; but his commitment as a father, husband, and health care professional came across in our conversation. I felt good about including his quotations in my article because sound spiritual values were evident even if not directly acknowledged.

Collect Clues

I'm not suggesting you snoop, but a little eavesdropping can't hurt! Pay attention to conversations around you. Listen for bits of advice. Ask questions and note the responses. Observe the way people behave. Notice the trivial as well as the essential. Every day is filled with useful clues that you can use in your writing. I turned table talk into many helpful how-to articles. "Are Your Children Over-Programmed?" resulted from a conversation with other mothers about the "lesson syndrome" in our society.

"Gratitude or Gossip: Change the Way You Relate at Work" sold to *Office Hours*, written after I listened to some women gossiping about their coworkers, low pay, and lack of appreciation. It was a spin-off of my Christian book *Basket of Blessings: 31 Days to a More Grateful Heart*. I didn't include any Scripture in the article but wove biblical themes throughout the piece: honoring one another, behaving with charity and compassion, being slow to anger, and giving thanks in all things.

I have also written personal opinion pieces and essays for secular newspapers in my hometown. I voiced my views about the population of homeless children in San Diego and what citizens can do to get involved in their lives. This manuscript was prompted by an article I read where the author took a strong stand against the homeless cluttering our community.

I also wrote an article about the ravages of mental illness in street people, triggered by memories of a close member of my family who was tormented for years with this condition. I didn't have any political, medical, or financial wisdom to offer. I simply encouraged people to do what my relative said she longed for during that unbearable season in her life: a kind word, a smile, a shared meal, a chance to talk and be listened to, or a walk hand-in-hand with someone who loved her.

This article gave me an opportunity to share the Beatitudes with readers without even mentioning them by name. People drop clues everyday in every way. When we are alert to them—both as writers and as Christians—we till the soil of our minds, plant seeds of faith and hope in others through our writing, and ultimately lay a foundation for the Gospel of Jesus Christ to reach readers in search of the truth.

No, we don't have to go to Africa, South America, or Borneo to fulfill the Great Commission. We have our own mission field as close as the touch of our computer keyboard. Writing for the secular market is not only an opportunity to grow as writers, it is an invitation to mature as Christians. It is a call on our lives and our talents that we cannot afford to ignore.

Tips for Writing for the Secular Market

- Clarify your goal. Decide what you wish to say, then choose a suitable market.
- Commit yourself to the project at hand. Focus your energy until you produce the result you want.
- Create an experience for readers. Give them one or more specific spiritual truths to use and apply in their lives. Promote action without preaching.
- Contact an editor with a solid query that outlines your article in detail.
- Complete the piece on time, bathe it with prayer, and pop it into the mail. Leave the result to the Lord.

Karen O'Connor is the author of thirty-five books; hundreds of magazine articles in both Christian and secular markets; and a popular writing teacher, consultant, and conference speaker. Karen served as the national language arts consultant for the Glencoe Publishing Company for four years and mentored many aspiring writers while teaching at the University of California Extension for fifteen years. She is currently an instructor with the Long Ridge Writers' Group and the editor of *Connections*, the school's newsletter for instructors. Contact Karen at 2050 Pacific Beach Drive #205, San Diego, CA 92109; phone/fax: 619-483-3184; e-mail: wordykaren@aol.com; Web site: www.karenoconnor.com.

— 10 —

Writing for the Educational Market

CINDI MITCHELL

The universe is made of stories, not of atoms.
—MURIEL RUKEYSER

MY DAUGHTER'S NEW FRIEND, Katie, squeaked open my office door and peeked inside. I was sitting on the floor surrounded by crayons, scissors, glue, and brightly colored pyramids that I made for my latest book *Dazzling Math Line Designs*. My daughter, Jeannine, grabbed her friend's arm and pulled her back into the kitchen. "Don't go in there," she whispered. "My mom is working."

Through the open door, I saw Katie's eyes widen, "What kind of work does your mom do?"

"Well, it's hard to explain," Jeannine said, as she took my science experiment from the refrigerator. "Do you want some *blood gelatin?*"

"It doesn't sound very good. Is it *really* made of blood?"

"No," Jeannine laughed. "My mom made it for work."

"I guess I'll try some," said Katie as she pulled out the kitchen stool and sat down. I stifled a chuckle as she jumped up quickly. "Yuck, what is this stuff?" she asked as she peeled green, slimy strings from the back of her legs.

"It's green slime. My mom…"

"I know. Your mom made it for work! But, what kind of work does she do?"

"She's a writer."

"Really? Why does she make all this weird stuff?"

"She writes books to give teachers ideas to try in their classrooms. Before she sends the ideas to her editor, she tries them out on us!"

"Cool," said Katie. "I wish my mom did that."

"Yeah, it's a great job—especially if you're an overgrown kid—like *my* mom."

Educational Writing—What Is It?

Whether you have children of your own, have formally taught, or are just an overgrown kid yourself, educational writing may be for you.

After twelve years of teaching in the elementary classroom, I was an unconscious expert on everything that had to do with prodding children to learn. I could turn a boring lesson on verbs into a game of Trashcan Baseball, teach fractions by making pizza, and demonstrate solar energy by cooking hot dogs in a homemade solar cooker. The problem was, I didn't think I knew a thing! I certainly didn't think I had golden nuggets of information the publishing world was dying to possess. Guess what? I was wrong.

When I met Terry Cooper, the editor-in-chief of Scholastic Professional Books, I saw myself as an ordinary teacher with a strong desire to write. She saw someone with a doctoral degree in practical teaching. What she knew about me, you need to know about yourself—you've been in the trenches with kids, you've wiped their noses, kissed their bruises, and taught them to read and write. A publishing company can get valuable information about successful teaching from you, and they never even have to pick out the Play-Doh™ from underneath their fingernails. You are the pot of gold at the end of the publishing rainbow.

I can hear your response. "Of course, *you* can write educational materials; *you* were an exceptional teacher. You have some special gift or talent I don't possess."

I have never met two educational writers who were the same. I know authors with Ph.D.s who write curriculum and textbooks, Sunday school teachers who write craft books and church curriculum, public school teachers who write classroom enrichment materials and short stories, and parents who write books about games and activities to play in a family setting.

The key to successful educational writing is to write what *you* know. Take your experiences with kids and share them. You don't have to be a teacher, writer, editor, or journalism major. The only real requirement is a strong desire to eat blood gelatin and play with green slime.

CHOOSING A TOPIC

There are ten or twenty publishers right now that would like to publish your teaching ideas. You need to figure out three things: which ideas to sell, which publishers are looking for your ideas, and how to write in a format acceptable to the publisher.

If you're like I was, you may not think you have morsels of truth to impart to the publishing world. In short, you don't think you have ideas to sell. Go to the Christian bookstore or teacher's store with a pencil and notepad. Look at the children's books. You'll find books about Bible crafts, chalkboard games, storytelling ideas, finger plays, animals in the classroom, Gospel talks, and more. When you see a topic you would like to write about or expand on, jot it down.

When I was in the bookstore, I saw beautiful books with butterflies, birds, and geometric designs for kids to color. Based on how much my fifth-grade students liked to color intricate designs, I knew this book would be a good seller. I wrote the idea on my notepad. Later when I was looking through my list of possible topics, I got this brainstorm: The perfect way to get kids interested in basic math computation was to put problems in gorgeous, three-dimensional designs they could color, based on the answers. My *Dazzling Math Line Design* book was born. Another way to get book ideas is to think back to successful teaching experiences you have had with kids. Maybe you used disappearing ink to explain to children that their sins were erased when Christ died for them, or you played Bingo with the Ten Commandments. Can you combine these experiences with new ideas to create a book?

When I was looking for a creative way to write a math word problem book, I thought back to one of my at-home teaching experiences. My son, Ben, received a science set for his birthday that gave us hours of family enjoyment, making and playing with gooey science creations. Based on that experience, I decided to write math word problems that, when solved, would give kids recipes for green slime, blood gelatin, bouncing balls, etc. I submitted the idea to a publishing house. They liked it so much they asked me to write a series of books using this theme.

Immerse yourself in the educational market by collecting catalogs (most publishing houses will send them free) and magazines. Talk to librarians, bookstore owners, teachers, or anyone who uses educational materials. Find out what kinds of materials they like and what topics they wish were available. Write down all these ideas.

After you've researched the market and looked at your experiences, generate a long list of possible book topics taken from all your sources. Allow yourself plenty of time so you can continue to brainstorm and add to the list. As you make your final decision on a book topic, keep this list of helpful hints in mind. Terry Cooper shared them with me when I was a beginning writer, and they have helped me sell over fifteen book ideas.

> Instructional books should make teachers' lives easier. Choose a book idea that will enhance the topics teachers are already required to teach.
>
> If you've never seen an idea similar to yours on the market, it probably won't sell. Writers don't need to reinvent the wheel. They need to write about topics similar to those already on the market but with a new, innovative twist.
>
> Books for kids need to include three basic elements: fun, fun, and fun!
>
> Study the publisher's catalog. Authors spend countless hours preparing to write a book that is currently on the market or is totally outside the realm of what the publisher wants.
>
> Write about what you love. Your enthusiasm for a topic will show in every word you write.

After you decide on a topic, the real work begins. You need to find the "perfect" publisher for your outstanding idea.

FINDING THE RIGHT PUBLISHER

I have talked with writers who have five-star ideas and brilliant proposals but never get their work published. Why? Because they didn't find the special publishing house that needed their product. Don't scrimp on this part of the plan. Do your market research, and do it well.

The most widely used children's market research guide in the secular world is the *Children's Writer's & Illustrator's Market*. Its counterpart in Christian publishing is the *Christian Writers' Market Guide* by Sally Stuart. They are both published yearly and are available at most bookstores and some libraries.

These guides include hundreds of companies that buy freelance material, complete with mailing information and names of the current editors. The listings are indexed according to publishers, age level, and subjects. Most listings include submission guidelines, contract and payment terms, and tips for getting published.

I study these guides carefully before I ever write a word. After I find four or five publishers that might want to publish a book about the topic I have chosen, I begin gathering information about the companies. I order their catalogs, look at books they have published, and talk to writers who have written for them.

Then I choose one target publishing house for which I want to write and buy several titles they publish. (Keep the list of other potential publishers. If your manuscript is rejected by your first choice, you can send it to the other companies.) I peruse these books from cover to cover and look at their formats and teaching strategies. Do they use a light, whimsical writing style or a serious, down-to-business tone? What teaching style does the company use? Do they publish cross-curriculum materials that include activities in reading, writing, art, drama, math, and science? Or do they prefer not to mix subject areas? On their student pages, do they use complex questioning styles that require essay answers, or do they use a simple fill-in-the-blank format? How many pages are most of their books?

After answering these questions and more, I am ready to tailor my book idea to match their other products. If my ideas deviate too much from the publisher's, I search for another target publisher rather than compromise the quality of my material.

Once you have finally chosen the best publisher for your material, it's time to take that last important step. Put your idea into a format acceptable to the publisher. Then write a query letter.

Writing the Query Letter and/or Book Proposal

When I started writing, everyone talked about queries; but I didn't know what a query was. A query is a letter of inquiry asking the publishing house if they would like to see a formal proposal outlining your book idea. Most queries include the following: a short letter stating your book idea, your qualifications to write it, and who your target audience is. If you get a go-ahead from the publisher to send the whole book proposal, include a cover letter (similar to your original query letter), a table of contents that briefly outlines your book chapter by chapter, and a completed chapter of your book and/or several examples of activities.

For additional information on writing queries, read *How to Write Irresistible Query Letters* by Lisa Collier Cool. This book shares practical advice on how to write a persuasive cover letter, how to best highlight your talents and background, and how to sell your ideas.

Liza Charlesworth, the executive editor of Scholastic Professional Books, and Virginia Dooley, a senior editor, have seen a million and one query letters. They outlined what makes a query sizzle and what makes one fizzle. Here are their thoughts.

Sizzlers

Simplistic proposals are the best. Give the editor a basic outline that can be reviewed quickly. To be honest, many queries are never read because they are too long and involved. Less is often more.

The sample activities in your proposal should be fun, exciting, and innovative. Kids today are constantly entertained. Dazzle them with your captivating ideas.

The sample activities should also be simple and easy to understand. Publishers know that teachers are busy; they won't spend fifteen minutes trying to understand the rules to a game.

Teachers have invaluable experience, and editors love working with them. Outline your experience working with kids.

If your ideas have been kid tested, let the publishers know. Editors look for ideas that teachers developed and used in the classroom.

Fizzlers

Sloppy work with typos is a sure candidate for the rejection pile. Edit your work several times and have a friend edit again.

Topics that are too broad or too narrow won't be considered. Keep in mind that most resource books are between 64 and 100 pages long.

Many proposals are dry and boring; the author is just rehashing an old topic with nothing to make it sparkle.

Know your markets. Look at the publishing house catalogs carefully. Believe it or not, Scholastic Professional Books gets queries on crocheting and dog care.

THE BEST-KEPT SECRET IN PUBLISHING

Now the waiting game begins. Your proposal is on an editor's desk, and you are waiting for that long-anticipated phone call to tell you your book idea has been accepted for publication. You wait, rehearsing the conversation between you and the editor.

At long last the phone rings, but the editor isn't calling to offer you a book contract. He is asking you questions about your proposal. Often the first call from an editor is little more than a fishing game. The editor is trying to figure out what kind of catch you are—a minnow or a twenty-pound bass. This isn't the time to act nonchalant and cool. Pour it on. Give it all you've got; sell yourself.

Al Christopherson is the vice president of publishing for Alpha Omega Publications, a Christian homeschool publisher. When asked what he is looking for in a new writer, he responded without hesitation, "Enthusiasm and commitment!" According to Mr. Christopherson, many writers have the knowledge and experience to write educational products. Yet only a few have the strong desire and zeal to deliver what Alpha Omega is hunting for—many quality products delivered on time year after year.

When the editor's voice is on the other end of the phone, don't forget the best-kept secret in publishing: Editors are looking for enthusiasm and commitment. They want to hear that you have so many book topics floating around in your head, you'll have to live to be 120 years old to complete them all. They want to know you are in writing for the long haul and you are bursting to write—especially for their company.

After the Contract

The editor decides you are the perfect person to write a book. Your heart sings, your mind soars, and you are ecstatic when you get the book contract. Then comes the inevitable. You put your fingers to the keyboard to write your book, and you are plunged into self-doubt. You don't think you are equal to the task. You wonder if the publisher has made a terrible mistake choosing you.

Don't panic. I have never talked to a writer who hasn't felt like this at one time or another. Just relax and start writing. Given time, these feelings will disappear; and you will regain your self-confidence. Remember, no one can write your book but you. It is a culmination of your experiences with kids. Write what you know, meet your deadlines, keep your promises, and enjoy being an author.

Educational Writing —What a Career!

After years of writing for children, there will be many books with your name on the cover. You may even lose sight of the remarkable career you established—until you receive a letter like the one below. My neighbor handed me this letter written for the school's "Career Week" by her-six year-old daughter, Page. The spelling has been improved for reading ease.

What I Want to Be When I Grow Up

When I grow up, I want to do what Mrs. Mitchell does.
She plays with green slime all day.
Blows bubbles and counts them.
Plays with measuring cups in the sand.
Colors pretty pictures.
Eats weird stuff.
She helps kids love to learn!

Page summed it up perfectly. Educational writers have a great job. They get to eat blood gelatin and play with green slime. But their greatest privilege of all is helping kids love to learn.

CINDI MITCHELL is a freelance writer and editor of educational and entertaining materials for children. She is the author of three math textbooks for grades four, five, and six and has written several teacher resource books for Scholastic Professional Books. Cindi lives in Mesa, Arizona, with her husband and two children. Visit Cindi's Web page at www.cindimitchell.com or e-mail her at Cindi@cindimitchell.com.

— 11 —

Writing Humor

JAMES N. WATKINS

Humor has the unshakable ability to break life up into little pieces and make it livable.

—TIM HANSEL

THE ASSIGNMENT FROM A MAGAZINE editor read, "The article needs to be very funny...with lots of humor."

Yah, right! Saturday my son and daughter decided to create a new Olympic event—the human shot put. Faith, then eleven, and our doctor's bank account won. Paul, seven, lost with a broken collar bone. Moments before, the word processing software went to where all good programs go when an electrical storm knocks out the power. Sunday, the same storm system drenched our church's outdoor community service.

That was followed on Monday by a visit to the dental hygienist who obviously attended the Marquis de Sade School of Dentistry. Tuesday, we sent our tearful daughter off to her first day of school in a new town. And then Thursday, the bank called to say our checking account was overdrawn.

It's hard to write something "very funny" when you feel like a deflated whoopee cushion. But it is possible as we'll see. And we'll also discover that nothing terrible ever happens to authors—just terrific anecdotes.

We have no better example of using humor to communicate effectively than Jesus Christ. Hyperbole or intentional exaggeration was the hip humor in that time. He would have had the crowds rolling on the hillsides with his comments about looking for a speck of sawdust in a brother's eye while having a plank in their own, camels squeezing through the eye of a needle, or religious hypocrites straining out gnats and swallowing camels whole. Jesus told stories that could only happen in cartoons. He even used ridiculous situations, such as putting a lamp (an open flame) under a bed (a flat, flammable mat).

When someone scolded Charles Spurgeon for using humor in his sermons, the late, great evangelist answered, "This preacher thinks it less a crime to cause a momentary laughter, than a half hour of profound slumber."

Likewise, the famous theologian G. K. Chesterton wrote, "I am all in favor of laughing. Laughing has something in it in common with the ancient words of faith and inspiration; it unfreezes pride and unwinds secrecy; it makes men forget themselves in the presence of something greater than themselves."

Purpose of Humor in Writing

To Connect with Your Readers

Could you relate to the week I described at the beginning of the chapter? We've all had those kinds of weeks and so—hopefully—a connection was formed. Hey, I guess my life doesn't have to be a laughing riot to write humor. Maybe I won't skip over this chapter after all.

To Comfort Your Readers

Best-selling humorist Barbara Johnson is a prime example of the concept that "comedy is tragedy plus time." Barbara has experienced more pain than most spouses and mothers; and yet she is able to write with wit and humor.

While I didn't find passing a kidney stone amusing at the time, here's how I began an article on pain:

> Everyone needs to have a kidney stone once in his or her life time. Preferably, the sooner the better.
>
> You see, experiencing the sensation of having a semi tractor-trailer with snow chains and a load of rolled steel park on your lower back tends to put life into perspective.

> For instance, if you're riding in a tour bus and the rest room door suddenly swings open and you can't reach the handle without creating an additional sight on the tour, you can say, "Hey, sure beats a kidney stone." (All of these examples are, of course, hypothetical and have never happened to me personally.) Or your daughter calls you at 1 a.m. in the middle of winter and says, "Gee, Dad, did you know that a '95 Neon can straddle a traffic island?" you can say, "Hey, sure beats a kidney stone."[1]

With humor, "we can comfort those in any trouble with the comfort we ourselves have received from God" (2 Corinthians 1:4).

To Confront Your Readers

Christ used humor to reveal his listeners' inconsistencies. German philosopher Arthur Schopenhaur claimed laughter is the "sudden perception of incongruity" between our ideals and our behavior.

For instance, here's the lead for an article on inconsistencies in the pro-choice arguments for abortion. (It's a touchy topic, so readers need some laughing gas before we start drilling away on the subject).

> We hear a lot about "pro-choice" on the evening news and sound bites from politicians. We, too, want to avoid "legislating values and claiming there are moral absolutes." Ethics is a personal choice, not a political or religious concern.
>
> That's why we've established "Planned Bank Robbery." Now, we personally don't approve of bank robbery, but we don't want to inflict our morals on anyone else either. We're "pro-choice" when it comes to grand larceny. It must be a personal decision of each individual.
>
> Education is the key since our studies reveal that 99 percent of senior high teens know that banks are robbed. But it is shocking the number of teens who don't know *how* banks are robbed. Or even how to load a .357 magnum, drive a get-away car, or demand, "Give me all of your unmarked, non-sequentially-ordered twenty-dollar bills." Young people need to know the wide range of career options available to them....

> And young people who need some extra cash from their local 7-11 shouldn't have to get their parent's permission to obtain this protection [such as a bullet-proof vest]. If that were the case, hundreds more teens would be needlessly injured by narrow-minded parents who are trying to inflict their morality on their children.
>
> Again, let me emphasize that "Planned Bank Robbery" does not condone or encourage grand larceny. We only want to stress it is a personal decision. We're "pro-choice"![2]

By taking a group's arguments and transferring them to another issue, we can point out the inconsistencies.

Sources for Humor in Writing

As I present this material at writers' conferences, someone—usually with a pocket protector filled with engineering pens—objects by saying, "But I'm not a funny person." I believe we all can hone our sense of humor if we heed the following suggestions.

Don't Take Your Situation Too Seriously

Christ reminds us in Matthew 6:25-34 not to worry about temporal things but to trust our heavenly Father. That gives us freedom to laugh at today's troubles. For example:

> I don't believe in paying a repair person $50 per hour when I can fix it myself. What do I have to lose? It's already broken, so I really can't do too much more damage.
>
> Such was the case with the "simple"—watch out for that word—task of removing the bathroom stool so the tile crew could install new floor covering. And I'd save $50 by doing it myself!
>
> First, I managed to break the main shut off valve to the house.
>
> *No problem,* I told myself. *I'll just call the water department to come out and shut off the water for an hour or two.* But then the thirty-year-old bolts magically transformed into little piles of rust when I tried to remove them from the base of the stool.

> *No problem. I'll just drill them out and run quarter-inch bolts straight through the bathroom floor.* This would have worked fine if there had been a bathroom floor. A slow leak under the stool had reduced the subflooring to the consistency of wet cardboard.
>
> Finally, our family gathered "around the throne" for a prayer meeting and a good laugh.
>
> "Tim Taylor didn't mess up his bathroom this badly, Dad!" my eight- and twelve-year-olds roared. I had to laugh, too.[3]

Greek theater divided plays into two categories: tragedies and comedies. Tragic tales had dire endings, such as the bountiful body counts at the end of many of Shakespeare's plays. In comedies, however, the hero and heroine always lived "happily ever-after" or at least had a pulse at the curtain call.

Romans 8:28 provides the ultimate punch line: "And we know that in all things God works for the good of those who love him, who have been called according to his purpose." It's sort of a good news/bad news joke. For instance, the bad news: The post office lost my airline tickets recently. But the good news: Due to a price war, the replacement tickets were $150 cheaper. God is able to take tragedy and turn it into a comedy in the Greek sense of the word. His powerful control of life provides the final punch line.

As Christians, we can learn to see the lighter side of most situations—or at least be consoled that someday they will make great testimonies, stories for family reunions, or illustrations for a book. So don't take your situation too seriously.

Don't Take Your Senses Too Seriously

Christ reminds us that "if your eyes are good, your whole body will be full of light. But if your eyes are bad, your whole body will be full of darkness" (Matthew 6:22-23). In other words, how we look at things determines our attitudes and actions.

Some people simply refuse to see the humor in situations. Their lives are filled with a dark seriousness. But a sense of humor can be developed. It can see beyond sight, hearing, touch, taste, and smell to detect all the interesting surprises, inconsistencies, and contradictions to which many people are blind and deaf.

For instance, while in a desperate struggle with an "easy-to-install" shelving unit—watch out for those words too—I asked my son, who was five-years-old at the time, for a yardstick. Five minutes—and one migraine headache later—Paul arrived lugging half a tree.

"What are you doing, Paul? I need a yardstick!"

He looked at me innocently. "But, Dad, it is a stick from the yard."

After several minutes of laughing and hugging, my headache was gone; and I was able to conquer the shelves with new enthusiasm. (According to William Frye at Stanford University, laughter actually causes our bodies to produce endorphins that are natural stimulants and pain killers that benefit circulation, respiration, the central nervous system, and our immunity system. Norman Cousins, past editor of *The Saturday Evening Post*, actually laughed himself well from a near fatal illness by watching "Candid Camera" reruns. Proverbs 17:22 is medically, as well as spiritually, true: "A cheerful heart is good medicine."

A large part of humor is looking at things from a slightly different perspective, so be sensitive to the funny things around you. The famous author Flannery O'Connor writes that Christianity is serious business that creates serious comedy. "Only if we are secure in our beliefs can we see the comical side of the universe."

Don't Take Yourself Too Seriously

Obviously, not everything is life is funny. We need to take our faith and our friendships seriously. But the rest of Proverbs 17:22 warns against taking ourselves too seriously: "a crushed spirit dries up the bones." The incredible amount of time and energy to keep up a dignified front and the unbearable pressure to perform perfectly squeezes the life and humor out of a person.

There is a deep-down joy as well as a confidence in God's control of our universe that gives Christians a real reason to laugh. And once we've learned to laugh at ourselves, we have a lifetime of humorous material.

Cautions of Humor in Writing

Use Humor to Help Not Hurt

While Christ used irony, satire, paradox, and hyperbole in his messages, we find no sarcasm or put-downs—except in Matthew

23. So unless you're the Son of God writing to Pharisees, avoid humor at others' expense.

Use Humor to Introduce or Reinforce a Point

Speakers are often guilty of telling a joke simply to get a laugh—or to keep the audience awake between points nine and ten. However, pointless humor simply distracts from the point we're trying to make. Ideally, when readers remember the humor, they remember our message.

Use Humor Discretely

Humor that is appropriate for *The Door* (Christianity's answer to *Mad*) won't be appropriate for *Moody*.

Use Humor Tastefully

A minister recently sent his e-mail pals this so-called joke. "What do you call a women with two black eyes? A slow learner." Don't even think about using ethnic, racist, or sexist humor.

Use Humor Sparingly

During high school I cooked homemade spaghetti sauce while my mother was in the hospital. I dutifully put in the required a quarter cup of garlic. Unfortunately, the recipe called for fresh garlic, not powered garlic. We had bad breath for two weeks.

Think of humor as seasoning that is lightly sprinkled throughout the article or book.

SECRETS OF HUMOR IN WRITING

Put the Punch Line Last

For instance, which of the following is more humorous? ("Neither" is not an option.) (1) "I'm critically acclaimed but commercially ashamed since my books have won awards but never a spot on the best-seller lists." Or (2) "My books have won awards but never a spot on the best-seller lists. I'm critically acclaimed but commercially ashamed."

The first example gives away the punch line. Remember, put the punch line or the unexpected twist at the end.

Use Details

Here's another pop quiz. I recently wrote an editorial on the importance of intolerance. Which is funnier? (1) "For instance, do you really want to go to a doctor who is tolerant? I want a doctor who is narrow-minded and completely intolerant to disease." Or (2):

> For instance, do you really want to go to an "open-minded" doctor with signs in the waiting room that read: "I Brake for Bacteria." "Save the Salmonella." "Take a Stand for Polio!" I want a doctor who is narrow-minded and completely intolerant to disease and physical afflictions when I'm told, "Turn your head and cough."[4]

The secret is in the details.

Work on Your Timing

Be sure you read your article or chapter aloud. Better yet, read it aloud for a writers' group. Timing is the secret to good stand-up comedy and sit-down writing.

Read Other Humorists

Patsy Clairmont, Liz Curtis Higgs, Barbara Johnson, and Laura Jensen Walker are just a few examples of Christian authors who use humor well. You're also welcome to visit my Web site at www.noblecan.org/~watkins for the "rest of the story" on the excerpts in this chapter.

The Apostle Paul wrote, "Let your conversation be always full of grace, seasoned with salt, so that you may know how to answer everyone" (Colossians 4:6). The word *salt* can also be translated "wit," or humor. Our world has its share of comedians and humorists, but it is in desperate need for humor that heals and redeems.

You can provide that "good medicine" of laughter.

Endnotes

1. Jim Watkins, "It sure beats a kidney stone," *Kendallville News-Sun* (November 3, 1977), p. A9.
2. Jim Watkins, "Planned Bank Robbery," author's Web site.

3. Jim Watkins, "We'll Laugh at This Someday," *Light and Life* (January 1990), p. 6.
4. Jim Watkins, "Intolerance not always a bad thing," *Kendallville News-Sun* (March 2, 1998), p. A9.

JAMES N. WATKINS is a freelance writer who speaks at camps, churches, and conferences throughout the United States and internationally. Jim is also a part-time instructor at Taylor University Fort Wayne. As an author, he has sold over 1,200 articles, devotionals, poems, reviews, scripts, short stories, and song lyrics, as well as over 100 color and black and white photos. His work has appeared in *Campus Life*, *The Christian Communicator, The Christian Reader, Christianity Today, Decision, The Door, Leadership, Moody, Today's Christian Woman, and War Cry*. His eleven published books include *Characters* (comedy/dramas, Lillenas), *Death & Beyond* (Tyndale), *The Persuasive Person* (Wesley Press), *Sex Is Not a Four-letter Word* (Tyndale), and *Should a Christian Wear Purple Sweat Socks?* (Wesley Press).

—— 12 ——

The Poet's Palette

MONA GANSBERG HODGSON

Poetry is a language that tells us, through a more or less emotional reaction, something that cannot be said. And it seems to me that poetry has two characteristics. One is that it is, after all, undefinable. The other is that it is eventually unmistakable.

—EDWIN ARLINGTON ROBINSON

DO YOU LONG TO CREATE artistic expression using emotional and rhythmical language? Do you desire to release what can only take flight on the wings of poetic expression?

William Wordsworth, Gerard Hopkins Manley, Robert Frost, Maya Angelou, and Luci Shaw convey a more profound message in 200 words than many prose writers do in 1,000 words. How do they do it? They are poets who learned to choose and blend words as Michelangelo arranged colors on his canvas. These poets create vivid images, choosing words that draw readers into their verse. And we can too.

Sherwood E. Wirt once said, "Poetry is an attempt to capture through rhythm and meter an aspect of truth that prose can never completely express. It is the concrete and artistic expression of the human mind in emotional and rhythmical language."

SENSE APPEAL

Sight. Sound. Smell. Taste. Touch. Drawing your readers into your poem involves the senses, evoking an emotional response.

Mary Harwell Sayler, one of my poetry mentors, pointed me toward the King James Version of the Bible, especially the Old Testament, to study the art of writing poetry that appeals to the readers' senses.

Read Job 6:2-4 and Job 7:4-5 in the King James Version. In these passages, Job describes his grief as being "heavier than the sand of the sea," saying his words were swallowed up. He also wrote, "the arrows of the Almighty are within me, the poison whereof drinketh up my spirit." He describes his flesh as being "clothed with worms and clods of dust."

Talk about vivid images! You can sense the pitiful condition in which Job finds himself. Would you experience empathy if he'd just said, "Boy, am I a mess?" We are compelled to empathize with him because our senses have been awakened.

For another example, take a look at my poem "Awakening."

> Concealed in midnight
> shadows, the dormant bulb sips
> life-granting water—
> waiting to debut a lit color-tipped stem in
> dawn's revelation.
> At the dawn of new
> beginnings, we bend and stretch,
> shaking off haggard
> yawns from darkening
> failures as we stretch toward God's
> fresh morning Sonshine.[1]

Hopefully, your senses were engaged and you identified with the bulb. Did you find yourself straining to see the light, sipping water from the soil? Did you stretch toward the light, as you waited for the results.

Try this exercise in sense appeal. On a blank piece of paper or on your computer screen, make a column for each of the senses. Go through the above passages in Job, looking for the words that indicate or infer one of the senses. Place the word or phrase that implies a sense in the appropriate column. After you've applied this study method to Job and to the work of your favorite poet, try it on one of your poems. Then ask the following questions:

Did I put any ingredients into my poetic pot that would stir the senses?

How many senses are implied in my work?

Can the readers smell, taste, see, hear, and touch my experience?

Can the readers relate to my experience as one of their own?

What words or phrases can I transform to help my readers see, smell, taste, hear, and touch my poem's message?

While a single poem may not contain references to or imply all of the senses, it should awaken at least one of them and create reader empathy for your experience or subject. Help your readers see what you see and feel what you feel through the use of sense appeal.

FIGURATIVE LANGUAGE

Metaphors, similes, and personification also help to create tangible word pictures for your readers. These techniques employ everyday experiences and observations to illustrate what could not otherwise be shown.

Metaphor

A metaphor implies a comparison by saying, "This is that." "God is my rock" and "love is a rose" are familiar examples. The words *like* or *as* aren't used in a metaphor.

For an example of metaphor usage in poetry, take another look at my poem "Awakening." While I don't say we are the dormant bulbs waiting for spring and new life, I do imply it. The metaphor permeates the poem with words and phrases like "concealed in midnight shadows," "dormant bulb sips life-granting water," "waiting to debut," "dawn of new beginnings," "shaking off haggard yawns from darkening failures," and "as we stretch toward God's fresh morning Sonshine."

Notice I didn't digress from the image of an incubating bulb. Study metaphors, then test your own. What image are you trying to project? Make a list of all the figurative words and phrases in your poem. Are they consistent with the image you are trying to bring into focus? If not, you still have work to do. Unless you're doing so to create a humorous effect, don't mix your metaphors.

Simile

A simile emphasizes a comparison, usually using "like" or "as." "Like a caged tiger, he paced and glared," "she is busy as a bee," and "he is hard as nails" are familiar examples.

In describing his vision in Revelation 1:12-16 (KJV), the Apostle John used many similes. He said he heard a voice and turned and "saw seven golden candlesticks; And in the midst of the seven candlesticks [he saw] one like unto the Son of man.... His head and his hairs were white like wool, as white as snow; and his eyes were as a flame of fire; And his feet like unto fine brass.... And his voice as the sound of many waters...And his countenance was as the sun shineth in his strength."

John used wool, snow, fire, brass, waters, and the sun to describe what he saw. When attempting to explain something in a simile, like John did, liken your object or feeling to something familiar to the readers.

Train yourself to see images, think about comparisons, and record them in a poetry notebook.

Personification

When employing personification, we attribute human characteristics to nonhuman or inanimate objects. The Bible is full of personification, especially in Psalms where hills clap their hands, the whole earth sings, and the heavens declare. In my poem "Awakening," the dormant bulb sipped.

In his poem "Daffodils," William Wordsworth appealed to our senses with his opening simile, "I wandered lonely as a cloud." The poem is also packed with personification. Daffodils toss their heads and waves dance.

Joyce Kilmer's poem "Trees" talks about a tree that "lifts her leafy arms to pray" and a tree that wears a "nest of robins in her hair."

Sound Effects

Sound effects can also help to draw your readers into your poem. Alliteration and homonyms tease the tongue and ear.

Alliteration

Alliteration is one of many ear- and eye-pleasing tools in your potential poetic palette. It is a repetition of sound either in consonants or vowels. Repeating consonants is most commonly used. The repetition of the letter *p* in "potential poetic palette" is alliteration.

My poem "Breakthrough" serves as an example of how I used alliteration in a poem.

God breaks through
chaos,
cries,
chatter
not with fiery
condemnation or
condescending concern
but with a whisper—
"I care.
I love you!
Come away,
spend time with me."
Replacing
chaos with gentleness,
cries with comfort,
chatter with communion
He speaks peace.[2]

Homonyms

Homonyms are words that sound alike when pronounced but have different spellings and meanings. Examples include: way and weigh, do and dew, feat and feet, dough and doe. I used a homonym in my poem "Excuses."

I would write, but
tea kettles scream;
pencils need sharpening;
telephones ring.
Time for excuses
always abounds,
even when the right time
to write isn't found.[3]

An appropriate homonym or two can also serve to awaken the senses.

Tips for Sensory Images

We've looked at some of the figurative colors you can use to draw your readers into your poems. Here are eight tips to help you create portraits from your own palette of picturesque words.

Draw from Your Senses

Become aware of your surroundings, using all of your senses. Carry a notebook or index cards, and record your discoveries. Here are some examples from my experience: a pigeon stepping off a curb, the pungent odor of burning weeds, the shrill sound of a cricket at 2 a.m., the pang of leaving my daughter at her university dorm for the first time, the sweet taste of kiwi, and the mushiness of an overripe banana.

Use Comparisons

When drawing on imagery, refuse to settle for the obvious or the dull. Avoid clichés. Keen senses can provide new comparisons. With your notebook in hand, use your imagination to make fresh comparisons between descriptions and concepts. Brainstorm, letting the ideas flow freely. Have fun. Take time to let new comparisons gel. Then go back and refine them later. Look for fresh ways to connect this to that.

What does a rainbow look like? Like a colored chalk drawing or a pastel afghan? How does the earth smell after a storm? Like a sweater pulled from a drawer with a freshening sachet or like a head of cabbage fresh from the garden? Use your senses to observe and compare. And record your musings.

Picture Where You Are

Allow your unique stance in life to permeate your poetic expression. Let your readers get to know you. Draw figurative examples from your situation and stage in life, as well as from your locale. Your family life, your work, your play, your hobbies can provide fresh imagery, helping readers to identify with you and experience your poem.

Use Specific Details

Search for the best words. Cut out unnecessary words. Rely on strong nouns and active verbs. In short, be concise.

We can't create sharp, mental images by using generalities. Bring your writing into focus, using specific details and description. Don't say "tree" when you can say "weeping willow" or "oak." One is wispy, the other is stout. Let specific detail contribute to your poem's tone and mood description.

Choose Words to Set Tone and Mood

Job staged a melancholy scene in accordance with his heavy spirit. But in Song of Solomon 2:10-13, Solomon describes a fresh season, one full of singing birds, blooming flowers, and trees bearing fruit. Solomon depicts a lighthearted mood with his word choices. The impact of their poems explodes when we identify with their emotions and experiences as our own.

Take a look at one of your poems. Do your word choices set a specific tone and mood? Or is there inconsistency? Is it the best tone and mood for your imagery and message?

Consider Your Readers

You'll write differently for children than you do for adults. And you may relate differently to other Christians than you would to non-Christians. Will your intended readers be able to identify with the figurative language you've chosen?

Read a Lot of Poetry

Get your hands on some poetry anthologies or collections. Anthologies give you the opportunity to taste a variety of forms and styles. Look for them in libraries, used books stores, and garage sales. Consume and digest a variety of forms and styles. Be sure to sample what is being published today along with past masterpieces.

Play with Words

Poets are freed by the very nature of poetry to play with words. Listen to words. You might want to make a list of words that intrigue you. Study words—their meanings and their nuances. Play with words and their relationships.

Sitting down to play with words is like standing in line at a potluck. You have lots of choices. There are so many new things to try. Be adventurous.

As is the case with any good seasoning, you'll want to sprinkle your figurative and playful pepper judiciously. Too much can cause your reader to sneeze and turn the page. But the right amount of a powerful spice in the perfect dish is like writing poetry with the Greats.

Endnotes

1. Mona Gansberg Hodgson, "Awakening," *Decision* (June 1997), p. 40.
2. Mona Gansberg Hodgson, "Breakthrough," *Decision* (February 1997), p 40.
3. Mona Gansberg Hodgson, "Excuses," *The Christian Communicator* (October 1992), p. 5.

Mona Gansberg Hodgson's poems have appeared in such publications as *Decision*, *Inklings*, *Campus Life*, *Living with Teenagers*, *Mature Living*, *War Cry*, *Standard*, *Purpose*, *Christian Living*, *Cross & Quill*, and *The Christian Communicator*. Her publishing credits include The Desert Critter Series (Concordia) and several hundred poems, articles, and short stories for adults and children in more than fifty periodicals. In addition to writing, teaching at writers' conferences, and speaking to women's groups, Mona serves as director of the Glorieta Christian Writers Conference in Glorieta, New Mexico. You may get in touch with her by e-mail at mona@sedona.net or at P.O. Box 999, Cottonwood, AZ 86326-0999.

— 13 —

Picture This! Writing the Perfect Picture Book

DANDI DALEY MACKALL

I try to write on my knees under the authority of God and at eye level with the child.

—CHRISTINE HARDER TANGVALD

YOU WANT TO WRITE A BOOK. How hard can it be? Kids should be easier to please than grown-ups, and the younger the better. Why not start with a picture book with big, beautiful pictures? Plus you only have to come up with a thousand words or less.

But if you've tried to write a picture book and get it published, you already know that creating picture book text is about as easy as squishing a pleasingly plump camel through the eye of a needle. Picture book authors have to capture—in a few, well-chosen words—character, theme, setting, tone, conflict, drama, humor, and surprise. So how does a picture book writer begin?

THE KERNEL

A good place to start the creative process is with the spark of discovery, the inspiration, the flash of insight. Call it the ah-ha or the fascination factor, the take-away or epiphany. Picture books move us. Great ones can touch the soul—without sermonizing.

A decade ago on Christmas Eve, my daughter asked, "Mom, does God have hands? I'd like to give Him a gift for His birthday, but I don't know if He can unwrap it." I knew I had a picture book kernel, and I wrote *The Christmas Gifts that Didn't Need Wrapping*. Another time as I passed a school, shouts of "Me first!" resounded from the playground. And I had my kernel for *Me First*, a story about mixed-up priorities.

Kernels are everywhere—in the world and inside of us. In fact, the kernel may be the easiest part of the creative process. We all have great ideas for picture books. But the idea itself, even a terrific idea, won't automatically make a picture book. You need a story.

Story First

Don't kid yourself into thinking a cute idea or a humorous situation can make a picture book. You have to transform that idea into a real, live story—with strong character development, a suspense-filled plot, and plenty of conflict, leading to a climax and a satisfying resolution. A story.

I learned the hard way about the need for a strong plot. In my first picture book, *The Best Christmas Ever*, initially I thought the idea would be enough: My character would give away the doll she loved most because God gave away His only Son. Only after I'd collected an embarrassing number of rejections did I give my character an inner conflict and a struggle with an antagonist.

One of the best ways to break into picture book writing is through writing Bible stories—for religious and mainstream publishers. But even though the Bible stories come loaded with action and drama, we have to choose an original slant and follow a story structure that works for kids.

When Landoll, Inc., asked me write its Christmas picture book, I knew there were hundreds of Christmas books on the market, all telling the same, wonderful story (that could never be improved on!). What I had to do was find my own slant. I focused on what Mary might have expected at each turning point in her life—a glorious wedding, a comfortable life. But in the end, she got much more than she expected.

Nonfiction picture book writers generally look for the stories that show the concept. Facts need to be transformed into revelations that can spark a child's imagination. In writing a book about bugs, I was amazed to discover how many billions of bugs exist in our world. But when I told my youngest daughter, her response was,

"Uh-huh." Finally I found a way to communicate that number so Katy would care: "If you dug up one square mile of dirt, you'd find more bugs than there are people in the whole world." I was rewarded with a "Wow!"

Find the story in whatever you write. Everybody loves a good story.

POINT OF VIEW

The single point of view may be one of the best-kept secrets among professional, published children's authors. If you want your child readers to identify with your main character and understand your plot and theme, master the art of the single point of view. Show your story through the eyes, heart, senses, and mind of a child. Filter every word through your viewpoint character.

If you're writing Christian or inspirational picture books, the single point of view is often your best way to communicate your theme. You certainly can't sermonize or leave your young readers with a finger-shaking moral of the story delivered by Mom or Grandma. But if you know how to take your readers inside your character's mind and heart, whatever your main character comes to realize, so will your readers.

Picture books need compelling and convincing characters, and a strong point of view can help you here too. Viewpoint provides the author an edge over television. We can invite our readers inside a character's mind to allow them to experience her innermost thoughts and desires. That's difficult to do in television, where the focus is on the external and visual action.

One of the series I wrote for Concordia Publishing House is The Puzzle Club Mysteries, 80-page novels for kids six to ten. Each time one of the mysteries is animated and turned into a TV special, I'm asked to write a picture book telling that story in a 32-page format. Those picture books are by far the hardest books I write! How can I get a 16,000-word story or a thirty-minute TV program into about 850 words?

After about 101 false starts on *The Puzzle Club Christmas Mystery*, I remembered my secret weapon—the single point of view. Although the TV special would show the three kid detectives fairly equally, I had to choose one—Alex—and show my picture book story through him. No matter how many spooky mansions or mysterious clues I included, my subtle message would have to come in the way Alex grew through the story.

Once you have your kernel, your story, and your point of view, it's time to face the first page of your book.

BEGINNINGS

Writing the opening of your picture book is an enormous task. Page 1 is a contract with your readers, a promise of the marvelous things to come. You have to hook your readers and make that page turn.

By the end of a brief first page, your readers should know what kind of story this is (genre and tone), where it's located (setting), whose story it is (main character and point of view), what's at stake (conflict and story problem), and the kind of writer you are (word choice and voice).

Nonfiction and concept books need to open with a similar contract. In a book called *The Four Seasons*, I wanted to promise the readers two things: (1) You'll learn about the seasons; and (2) There will be fun along the way. Here's how I began: "Once, a long, long time ago—Please don't ask the reasons—Someone took the whole, wide world and split it into seasons."

Usually it's a good idea to start in the middle of a story, rather than in the beginning, because that's where the action is. But in a tiny book called *God Made the World*, I began with the drama of creation:

> Before the beginning,
> There was no blue sky.
> No plants and no people,
> And nothing to buy!
> Then God said the word.
> He said, Let there be light!
> And out of pure nothing,
> God made day and night.

Now that's action! Some beginnings are just too good to pass up.

ENDINGS

There are as many possibilities for ending picture books as there are picture books. But when you write for children, save something for the end. Kids love surprises.

One type of ending is the circular ending. Bring your readers back to the familiar beginning, coming full circle like the prodigal son. In *All Things That Go*, after introducing all the standard vehicles, I ended:

> So take a tractor, truck, or train,
> Subway, spaceship, skates, or plane.
> 'Cause no matter **how** you roam,
> Things that go, can come back home!

In *My First Book of Time*, I started: "Six o'clock! Rise and shine! Time to wake up, Porcupine." You can guess where the book ends: "Eight o'clock! Time for bed! Close your eyes, you Sleepyhead."

Other endings deliver a punch line, a twist of plot, a play on words, a hint of irony, or a taste of eternity—pointing readers to the bigger picture. But with children, we have to make sure we don't drop in anything totally new. Prepare your readers for your ending before you get there.

GETTING THE PICTURE

Unless you're a professional illustrator, it's better to market your words alone. We all know wonderful author/illustrators who pull off great picture books. But what if the editor loves your text but isn't sold on the illustrations? You'll get the rejection on both. In general, it's easier to sell your text without pictures.

For most of us, writing a picture book is like coauthoring with an invisible partner—your illustrator. As the author, you must think visually, in scenes.

Again, I learned the need to think like an illustrator through my own humiliating experience. My editor returned a picture book manuscript to me with this question: "If you were the illustrator, what would you draw for the first three pages of your story?"

The obvious and humbling answer revealed that all three illustrations would have depicted the same scene—one character decorating the Christmas tree. Don't do that to your illustrator (or to your readers for that matter).

Keep in mind that an artist will create pictures that illustrate your text. Spend the few words you're allowed in the right places, showing your story and evoking details your illustrator can't capture. Don't waste words on colors and descriptions the readers can pick up in a glance at the illustration. Instead, convey smells and sounds, taste and touch, character thoughts, and dialogue.

It may help you to put together a dummy book or storyboard, cutting and pasting your text on each of the 27-29 pages. Pay attention to 2-page spreads (the left and right pages which will appear together in a book). Do they go together? Are you ending the right-hand page with enough of a cliff-hanger to make your readers turn to the next spread?

Each page of your book deserves a distinctive illustration. If your whole story can easily unfold with just a picture or two, you may have a magazine story instead of a picture book.

Finally, pay attention to language. That's how you create your own images in the readers' minds. A picture may be worth a thousand words—but not your words.

Technicalities

So you have your inspiration, your story angle, a great plot with a classic character, and a theme that will change lives and reach the world. How do you package it to capture an editor?

Word Count

How many words do you need for a good picture book? Fewer than you have. Cut every unnecessary word. Classic picture books run about 750 words. And in general, the shorter the better. Ordinarily, picture books run 32 pages long, using from 26-30 pages for text, with zero to a few lines of text per page.

Target a publisher and analyze the books they produce. Then make yours fit the line. Mark Plunkett of Standard Publishing confided to me years after he bought my first picture book that my research had paid off. When *Jenny's Christmas* came into his office, it joined a stack of unsolicited manuscripts on his desk. Unlike the others, my manuscript had just the right word count and fell into exactly 29 segments, the same as his Happy Day line.

"As I picked yours up," Mark admitted, "I hoped it would work because I didn't have much time to edit." Getting the technicalities down won't make an editor buy your manuscript. But it can't hurt to have an editor *want* yours to work!

Categories

Study the formats and target the right publishers. Besides the large, classically illustrated picture book, check out the 8x8s (i.e., Golden Books), concept books (numbers, alphabet, colors, time), board books (made of sturdier pages for baby wear and tear), pop-up books, and manipulatives (books that do something).

Submission

Check individual publisher guidelines because not all agree on this point. In general, type your text in normal paragraph form, perhaps leaving extra white space between what you see as page breaks. Don't send in 29 actual pages, but number each page as you would any manuscript. Indicate in your cover letter your word count and age level.

Illustrations

Unless it's absolutely necessary, don't tell the illustrator his or her job. Your illustrator needs the freedom to create too. Don't describe pictures you envision unless that illustration is essential, such as a visual joke or a wordless page. Do the best you can with words and leave the illustrating to illustrators.

Rhyme

You may have heard that a rhyming children's book is the hardest to sell. Unfortunately for all the would-be Dr. Seusses, it's true.

Children love good rhythm and rhyme. But editors receive so many manuscripts with poor rhyme that they have trouble giving any rhyme a chance. Before you try to sell rhyming text, see if your rhyme plays by the following rules:

1. Don't use off-rhyme. Rhyme means the same sound on at least the last syllable of two or more words. These words rhyme: *stay*, *day*, *okay*, and *obey*. These words don't: *say* and *days*, *again* and *gain*, *win* and *when*. Near-rhyme isn't nearly enough.

2. Match your meter. Study poetry and learn how to scan verse and identify poetic feet. You need the same metrical pattern, a series of matching accented and unaccented syllables.

Scanning may sound too technical, but it's the only way to make sure any readers can pick up your book, read your rhyme aloud, and make it work. (You can always make it sound right because you know just where to slide in that extra syllable.)

3. Don't use unnatural wording. Just because you're trying to get the rhyme, don't forget the importance of each word in your story. Never invert word order or give in to unnatural phrasing: "...the bird with a beak. / ...of which I do speak." You'd never say, "of which I do speak" in any other kind of story, so don't say it in a rhyming one.

4. Vary the rhymes. Rhymes quickly become tiresome unless you come up with unusual rhymes. Anybody can rhyme *day* and *way*. But you might need a good rhyming dictionary to come up with *ridicule* and *vestibule*.

5. Keep the story first. Your rhyme is only as good as the content, the story. Spend as much time crafting your story as you would if it didn't rhyme.

Writing a picture book may make that job of crafting silk purses out of sows' ears look easy. And when publishing budgets get cut, the first thing they'll consider getting rid of are those expensive children's books with the four-color illustrations.

But writing for our youngest readers is worth it all. Imagine a child sitting in Mom or Dad's lap, looking at your book as your words are read. And as your story is told, God uses those words to touch a family and draw them closer to Him.

So as you labor over that picture book, reach inside to the child in you and pull out your best. Your story might bring to life that secret child world and help you reveal the childlike faith Christ praised.

Get the picture?

Dandi Daley Mackall has published over 150 books for children and 28 books for adults. Her publishers include Prentice-Hall, Simon

Schuster, Tyndale House, Broadman & Holman, Harold Shaw, Concordia, Standard, Honor Books, Augsburg-Fortress, Landoll's, Prima/St. Martin's, Disney, and Hanna-Barbera. Her picture books include *God Loves Me*, *Picture Me With My Friend Jesus*, *Jesus Loves Me*, *The First Christmas*, and *The Puzzle Club Easter Adventure*. Her novels for kids six to ten include The Cinnamon Lake Mystery Series and The Puzzle Club Mystery Series. Her new middle-grade series, Horsefeathers, will be released this year by Concordia, and she's working on a series of picture books for Broadman & Holman. She writes from rural Ohio, where she lives with her husband and three children. You may contact her through Concordia or see her work in the Puzzle Club section of the Web site at www.lhm.org.

— 14 —

Step into Writing Beginning Readers

NANCY I. SANDERS

Reading is the primary tool of learning.
—LEE WYNDHAM

"I CAN READ!" RYAN ANNOUNCED triumphantly to his first grade teacher, Miss Lojas.

"He can read!" Miss Lojas said proudly to Ryan's parents at their midyear conference.

To prove her point, Miss Lojas handed Ryan a small, thin paperback. Ryan began to read aloud. Slowly, but surely, he turned page after page, reading the short words correctly.

The book Ryan used is commonly known as a beginning reader. A beginning reader is a story children read by themselves even though they're just learning to read. These stories range from books featuring one word per page to magazines including mini-stories with controlled vocabulary. They go on up through different levels to include first chapter books, the first books kids read on their own with chapters and whose entire book length equals roughly the same size as a chapter in a novel.

Beginning readers established a credible place in the publishing market because kids read them by themselves, and educators as well as parents want their children to read. As simple and basic as these stories appear, however, I've found it's very difficult to get published in this genre if the correct approach isn't followed.

Beginning readers fit into specific levels, formats, and guidelines. They're often used in the educational field under strict standards. Authors who want to prepare manuscripts for children learning to read through these step-by-step stories benefit from following a step-by-step approach to writing them.

Step One: Begin with Prayer

Whether we write for the Christian or secular market, whether we tell stories about Jesus or addition facts, as Christian authors of children's stories we represent God and His precepts to impressionable young minds. Every story we write and every project we work on needs to be started and continued with in prayer.

Step Two: Research the Market

The secular market has a large variety of beginning reader series. Each publisher uses a unique method of dividing its series into age and reading levels. Each beginning reader series follows a specific format according to the number of pages it contains, the grade level of vocabulary words it uses, the maximum number of words it has in each sentence, and the total word count in the entire book. You can find out the specific requirements each publisher has for its beginning reader series by studying its books in the bookstore and sending for writers' guidelines.

The Christian market is in the process of building a stronger book market for beginning readers. Beginning readers in the Christian market don't sell the volume the secular market sells, simply because secular publishers target a prolific buyer the Christian market doesn't have: the public school.

The market for beginning readers is not limited to books, however. There is a need for stories written for beginning readers in such publications as Christian and secular children's magazines, Sunday school take-home papers, and teacher-resource books featuring reproducible story pages.

Step Three: Choose a Publisher

After you spend a valuable amount of time researching the current market for beginning readers, choose one publisher for whom you would like to write a manuscript. By the time you've spent hours propped uncomfortably in the tiny chairs of the children's section, digesting beginning readers to the accompaniment of squawking babies and tousling siblings, you'll probably know which publisher's stories you like the best. Perhaps they're the ones that make you giggle like the seven-year-old sitting next to you who's reading a silly book. Or maybe they're the ones found in a well-worn magazine the kids couldn't keep their hands off. Whether you want to write a beginning reader story for a curriculum publisher, a children's magazine, or a book publisher, request writers' guidelines and a sample issue or catalog of their product line. If the publishing house accepts unsolicited manuscripts, carefully study their entire product line to get a knowledgeable feel for the type of literature they publish. Then focus on their beginning reader section. Determine which levels they publish and don't publish. Consider whether you should try to fit into an already existing series, or if you should propose a new series of your own.

If you opt to propose a new series, make sure it matches the same age level and reading level of an existing series the company publishes. Companies may be willing to publish a new idea for a reading level they already market, but they usually won't publish a new author in a series for an age level or reading level they don't already list in their catalog.

STEP FOUR: FOCUS ON ONE LEVEL OF BEGINNING READERS

Do you want to write a first chapter book? Do you want to write a thousand-word beginning reader story with a second grade vocabulary level for a children's magazine? Do you want to write a story for children ages three to six with a controlled vocabulary level of preschool through first grade with words that can easily be recognized?

Choose which level of beginning reader you want to prepare for the publisher for whom you'd like to write. Collect samples from that publisher that are written for this specific level. Read these stories over and over, studying them carefully, until you feel like you know this product inside and out.

STEP FIVE: CHOOSE A THEME OR TOPIC

Now you're ready to choose the theme or topic for your story. Again, you'll be using the publisher's catalog and sample material to guide you in your decision.

Does the publishing house feature stories based on a typical day in school? Do most of their stories teach a moral or a value lesson? Do they use nonfiction or strictly fiction? Determine a common thread among the titles of their stories—and then look for a unique angle that hasn't yet been covered.

Step Six: Use Fiction Techniques

I attended a class at a writers' conference on fiction techniques, even though I only wrote children's books at the time. It was one of the best things I ever did as a writer. Among other things, I learned about character development, plot synopsis, and setting. Fiction techniques are invaluable tools even when writing a beginning reader with only 500 words.

Before you write a single word, make sure you prepare for your story by developing characters, plot, and setting that jump off the pages and grab young readers.

Step Seven: Write Your Story

You're finally ready to write. You've studied the markets and used fiction techniques to prepare for your story. It's time to write. Sit down in your chair, fasten your seat belt, and write. Don't worry about how it sounds or what it looks like at this point. There will be enough time for editing later. Click into your creative mode, follow your notes, and write the story from beginning to end.

Step Eight: Check, Edit, and Revise

The first thing I do after writing a beginning reader story is to pull out my copy of *Children's Writer's Word Book* by Alijandra Mogilner. An essential reference tool for anyone writing for this market, this book lists vocabulary words taught from kindergarten level to sixth grade. It labels at which grade level each word is taught, and also describes the types of sentence structure and comprehension level each age level of elementary child is expected to know. It also contains a thesaurus with related words labeled according to grade level.

Using this book, I look up every word in my manuscript, checking for words that are too advanced. I also make sure each sentence contains the appropriate number of words for the age level for which I'm writing. For example, if I'm writing a beginning reader for first and second graders, I circle every sentence that is longer than seven words. I also circle every word in my manuscript that is for third graders or older. I then shorten sentences and replace as many words as possible with words taught in kindergarten through second grade.

Sometimes, however, I need to keep a certain word in the story because there aren't any lower-grade synonyms that fit. When I wrote *Marshal Matt and the Case of the Secret Code*, I saw the word *code* was a third-grade word. Since I needed it to carry the plot, I repeated the word several times throughout the text. This helped young children learn to read the new word. I kept these advanced words at a minimum within the manuscript, though, always repeating them if I absolutely needed to keep them in the story. This is how I developed what is known as a "controlled vocabulary" within the manuscript text.

After I check to make sure the manuscript meets the qualifications of the specific level of beginning reader I'm writing for, I put it through strenuous editing and revisions. Finally, I take my manuscript to a critique group or ask other writer friends to edit it again. I polish and revise the manuscript until it flows well.

STEP NINE: PREPARE TO SUBMIT THE MANUSCRIPT

My typical submission for a beginning reader's manuscript usually contains the following: a cover letter, my résumé, a résumé extension, and the manuscript.

A cover letter is simply a query letter that accompanies a manuscript. In the cover letter, it's good to begin with an upbeat line of text from your manuscript to catch the editor's eye. Follow this introduction with an explanation of your manuscript theme. Pinpoint into which reading level and age level your manuscript fits, using the exact terms this particular publishing house uses. Then describe how your manuscript fills a niche in a specific area of the publisher's marketing list. Finally, briefly introduce your writing credentials, trying to keep the letter limited to one page. Regardless of whether my résumé fills a separate sheet of paper or is simply a paragraph on the cover letter, with the submission of a beginning reader manuscript I always try to include what I call a résumé extension.

The résumé extension is a separate sheet of paper with my name and address at the top. Next it has a sentence or two for the editor, such as: "I would be interested in writing beginning readers on a variety of topics. If any of the following topics might fit into your publishing plans, please mark it and indicate for which reading level you would be interested in reviewing a potential manuscript."

Following this brief letter, I make a check-off list with five to twenty topics I think would interest the editor, drawing from my research of the publisher's catalog. A friend once recommended I include this separate sheet, and I have gotten contracts from topics on these lists even though my original manuscript was rejected.

Prepare the manuscript a final time for submission, making sure to follow the proper format for a children's manuscript proposal. If it's a story for a magazine, the format appears in running text. If it's a book proposal, however, the text needs to be divided into pages and spreads, much the same way a picture book manuscript is prepared. Because a beginning reader often uses few words, it's appropriate to include illustration suggestions as needed to help the editor/artist understand the story line.

Step Ten: Submit Your Manuscript, and Start on Your Next Project

If you've never before published a beginning reader, plan to work from three months to one year on preparing your manuscript up to this point. If you take less than three months, you're probably not spending enough time doing such necessary things as thoroughly researching the markets or revising your manuscript. If you take longer than a year, chances are you're not giving enough serious effort to this manuscript; and it will become overwhelming and unbearable, seemingly more difficult than it should be. In both cases, a rejection is likely to return in the mail.

When your manuscript is finally ready for submission, put your entire manuscript packet into an unused envelope, include your SASE, and send it off. Take a walk around the block, go shopping, visit a friend, and then start on your next writing project. The task of processing manuscripts at a publishing house usually takes at least three months, and the competition is fierce. If you're well on your way into writing your next story by the time you hear back from the editor, the rejection will be easier to take or the acceptance might open the door for submission of your current project.

Writing beginning readers is fun. It can also be very rewarding. I'll never forget the afternoon I stood browsing in a discount store at the book racks. A mother breezed past, pushing her child in a shopping cart when her son squealed with excitement. "What is it?" she asked, braking her cart to a stop.

Her son pointed to a children's book and exclaimed, "I just learned how to read that book today in kindergarten! I want it!" Without a moment's hesitation, the mother plucked the book off the shelf, handed it to the little boy, and headed on down the aisle. I listened to her child crowing with delight as he turned the pages of his very own beginning reader, carefully sounding out the words.

Writers of beginning readers share the awesome privilege of teaching children how to read. When children learn to love reading because of our work, we've introduced them to a love of the written word. As they grow older, God channels this love of reading into a desire to read His Word. As a writer, this is rewarding indeed!

Nancy I. Sanders enjoys writing beginning reader stories for Sunday school curriculum, children's magazines, and teacher resource books. She has authored over twenty books and is a contributing editor of *The Christian Communicator*. Her craft ideas have appeared in *Better Homes & Gardens'* "BH&G KIDS!" and on their Web page. Nancy is currently working with Scholastic Professional Books on a reproducible math book geared for beginning readers. You may reach her via e-mail at JNDBSand@juno.com.

—— 15 ——

Writing Truth to Teens

Bob Hostetler

The world will never starve for want of
wonders, but only for want of wonder.
—G. K. Chesterton

Today's teenagers have all been born since Ronald Reagan was elected President. Most of them have never bought a vinyl record or watched a drive-in movie. They can't remember a world without AIDS, MTV, and computers.

The Christian who hopes to write for teens faces a challenge, not only because the world has changed so much in recent years, but also because there is no more effective age for influencing people for the Cross and the Gospel than teenagers. According to research, "about three-quarters of all people who have consciously, intentionally and personally chosen to embrace Jesus Christ as their Savior did so before their 18th birthday."[1] Thus, the Christian man or woman who seeks effectiveness and efficiency in the ministry of writing may choose no better mission than writing for teens.

As in all ministry, however, the desire or the call is not the end but only the beginning of the task. Just as a missionary to Brazil must undertake the study of Portuguese and a hospital chaplain should learn how to minister effectively to the sick, dying, and bereaved, so a writer must learn what it takes to write truth to teens.

So, while the following ten commandments for writing truth to teens are not exhaustive, I offer them as a starting point.

1. Thou Shalt Know Thy Audience

Most writers for teens are not teens themselves. This may be obvious, but it's an important point, nonetheless. I was thirty-four when my first book for teens was published (it has since sold 200,000 copies). How can a thirty-four-year-old or fifty-four-year-old (or a twenty-four-year-old, for that matter) write effectively for a teen audience?

One word: homework. Writers for teens must study their audience. They must observe how today's teens talk and walk; what they watch on television and listen to on the radio; how they dress; how they act when they're afraid, embarrassed, or excited; how they get up in the morning.

For example, in my teen novel, *They Call Me A.W.O.L.*, I wrote a scene in which the teen protagonist stumbled out of bed in the morning; shuffled to the kitchen for a glass of orange juice; and then returned to the bedroom where he sat on the edge of the bed, head bowed, eyes closed, while sipping his juice. An early editor noted on the manuscript page, "This is exactly how my teenage son gets up in the morning!" It was a small thing, but I was delighted that the details rang true.

Of course, some writers have the luxury (though they've probably never thought of it quite that way) of having teen children to study. But whether you have teen children or not, it will take homework to know your audience. That might mean eavesdropping on teens at the mall or movie theater or absorbing the activity as students change classes at the local high school. (If your children don't attend the school, call ahead for the principal's permission.) Or volunteer as a Sunday school teacher or Girl Scout leader. Carefully frequent teen chat rooms on the Internet. Subscribe to magazines like *Brio*, *Breakaway*, and *Campus Life*; and read some of the others at the library. (Be warned, however, that some secular teen magazines contain shockingly explicit material.)

Also, advises Teresa Cleary, a frequent contributor to such magazines as *Brio* and *Teenage Christian*, "Keep diversity in mind. Remember that not every teen reading your work will be a middle-class, white, Midwestern girl. Ask yourself, 'Does my story or article work for inner-city kids as well as suburban or rural kids? For Hispanic? African-American? Asian?'" You'll often discover a new richness arise in your writing as you begin to address such questions.

2. Thou Shalt Love Thy Audience

When I was an editor of a teen magazine, I received dozens of manuscripts every day from would-be writers for teens. Too often, however, those stories and articles revealed the author as someone who did not like teenagers much.

I especially remember one story, which featured a thirteen- or fourteen-year-old girl as a main character. This girl never uttered a kind word in the story. She treated everyone around her with contempt. Not only that, but the other teens in the story weren't much better. It was obvious to me (and it would have been obvious to a teen reader if the story had been published) that the writer of that story wasn't fond of teens.

Don't try to write for teens unless you absolutely love them, unless they make you laugh, unless you enjoy spending time around them—watching them, listening to them, and talking to them. That way, not only will your research be more pleasant, but your writing will be more attractive.

3. Thou Shalt Not View Writing for Teens As an "Apprenticeship" until Thou Gettest "Good Enough" to Write for Adults

It has happened at nearly every writers' conference I've attended. Someone will express an interest in writing for teens. "Why?" I'll ask, my eyes sparkling. "What makes you want to write for teens?"

"Well," comes the answer, "I really want to write for adults, but I don't think I'm ready for that."

In response, I'll usually say something like this: "If you really want to write for adults, I suggest you go for it. Because writing for teens is *not* easier than writing for adults. In fact, in some ways it's much harder and more demanding. But more importantly, as a Christian, you should write for teens out of a desire for God to use you, not out of a hope that you can apprentice as a teen writer until you get good enough to do something else."

In other words, the work of God is no stepping stone.

4. Thou Shalt Choose Thy Subject Carefully

No one wants to write what no one wants to read (go ahead, read that sentence again—it won't hurt my feelings). And yet sometimes we writers approach a subject or an idea with little thought for whether our intended audience will want to read our work when it is finished. This is especially true, it seems, among would-be writers for teens.

Editors of teen magazines are inundated with decent writing on topics that are of no interest to teens. Sure, teens need to respect adults; but are they likely to read an article entitled "Why You Should Respect Adults"? Of course not, because that's not a highly interesting subject to a teen. They might, however, read something about how to get along better with their parents because that's a need they recognize already, without an adult pointing it out to them.

What are the subjects that interest teens? Dating, of course, and anything about relationships with the opposite sex. Fashion and beauty. Friends and popularity. Sports. Music. Celebrities. But those aren't the only subjects that interest them.

For example, most kids don't want to read about apologetics; but they do want *answers* to their questions about God, Jesus, the Bible, and Christianity. They might pass over an article on health, but they would be interested in learning how to look and feel their best. A story about prayer might interest some, but something about how to pray more effectively for their friends would hit them where they live. They like to read about other teens but in a way that deals honestly with teen struggles and problems, rather than presenting this or that teenager as a perfect son, daughter, athlete, student, or Christian.

If you wish to write for teens, it will be important to write what teens need to hear by applying truth to the topics that matter most to them.

5. Thou Shalt Treat Teens with Respect

Another qualification for writing for teens is the ability to treat teens respectfully. One way to do this is by taking them—and their concerns—seriously. That means, for example, that teens' concerns about their personal appearance (i.e., whether their clothes are cool or what to do when acne strikes) are not silly or trivial. In teen culture, such things can have severe ramifications; and learning to deal with them can assume great importance.

Treating teens with respect will also mean avoiding unflattering or unrealistic characterizations of teens. It will mean examining and eliminating thinly veiled motives, scare tactics, or exaggeration. Respect will also mean not condescending, not preaching, and not hitting teen readers over the head with a moral or an application.

In the words of teen writer Teresa Cleary, "Be real. Life for teens today isn't all 'happily ever after'; and they typically don't go around quoting Scriptures to each other. Write about real problems that sometimes don't have easy answers. They'll appreciate you for it."

6. Thou Shalt Beware of Trends and Slang

Judging from the comments of magazine editors in Sally Stuart's *Christian Writers' Market Guide*, the inappropriate or ineffective use of slang is a problem among writers for teens. "Avoid slang," suggests one editor while a couple others say, "Don't use a lot of slang." Slang is a mine field. Teen writers must suggest the way teens talk while avoiding words and phrases that might be passé before the magazine or book is published. A good rule of thumb is to use only those slang expressions that have already stood the test of time. For example, "Gnarly, dude!" died a well-deserved death years ago; but "excellent," "awesome," and "cool" are pretty durable when used in the right way.

Beware, too, of incorporating the latest trends into your writing. Everyone may be wearing tie-dyed clothes this year, but by the time your book, story, or article comes out, that style may be gone. Or a certain brand of tennis shoes may be cool at your school; but a few hundred miles away, they may be considered geeky. In such cases, it's better to play it safe and dress your characters in styles that endure.

"Nor should you use the real names of movie, television, or rock stars," says Emily Costello in *Writer's Digest*. "They disappear (or disgrace themselves) faster than you can save the words on your word processor."[2]

7. Thou Shalt Use Humor

Just the other night at the dinner table, my fifteen-year-old son described a friend in his high school. "He hasn't always been a 'freak,'" he said, referring to one of the cliques at his school. "He's like a convert to 'freakism.'"

"What did he convert *from?*" I asked.

His reply was quick. "Preppie-anity."

Teens love a good joke or witticism. And anyone who wants to write for teens will need to sprinkle his or her writing with a generous dose of humor. Even the most casual look at the youth sections of bookstores will reveal the importance of humor in writing for teens; titles such as *I Don't Remember Dropping the Skunk, but I Do Remember Trying to Breathe*; *Don't Check Your Brains at the Door*; and *You're Grounded for Life! And 49 Other Crazy Things Parents Say* illustrate the appeal of humor to teen readers.

"But I'm no comedian," you might say. You don't have to be. Just learn what makes teenagers laugh—and what makes them groan (aim for the former, not the latter). Practice looking at things through their eyes. Imagine how parents, gym teachers, cafeteria personnel, and other adults sound to a teen. Use surprise, exaggeration, and unlikely combinations to build humorous situations. And remember that humor always works best when it has an element of truth.

8. Thou Shalt Keep Things Interesting

The rise of electronic media—television, movies, video games, computer games, and services—has made "stimulation addicts" of many teens. Media has affected their attention spans too. "Movies and television," says youth group leader Denny Adams, "change images every couple seconds; and kids' minds get used to that. As a result, they can sometimes find it difficult to focus on a given project for a long period of time. They're easily bored, and they're not willing to wait for results."

The youth writer must keep this "boredom factor" in mind as he writes. "This means," says Mike Yorkey, former Editor-in-Chief of Focus on the Family's teen magazines, *Breakaway* and *Brio*, "you have to stand on your head a little bit. For example, the lead has to be absolutely gripping: clever, funny, *different*. The great thing about that, though, is that there are virtually no rules. You can have fun with it, run with it, and get into an article or story almost any way you want to. You can let your hair down. BUT you need to pay attention to how long you spend on any given point because you'll need to get on to the next point pretty quickly."

9. Thou Shalt Seek Help

No, not the psychiatric kind (though, if you're interested in writing for teens, it might not be a bad idea). But you'll also want to seek help from several important sources.

The most fruitful source of help is likely to be teens themselves. Develop the habit of field-testing your writing: Enlist several teens to read what you've written, and ask them to be brutally honest. Ask them to evaluate your topic and your writing. Is it sufficiently interesting? Did it get boring at any point? Did any of it sound corny or unrealistic? Were the attempts at humor effective? If you were writing it, how would you change it?

Study the teen/young adult section of *Christian Writers' Market Guide* to learn what editors are looking for—and what mistakes they warn against. Subscribe to *The Christian Communicator*, *Advanced Christian Writer*, and *Writer's Digest* or *The Writer*. Join a writers' group in your area. Check out Christian writers' conferences and take classes and workshops on writing for teens. Search the Internet for online Web sites, chat rooms, and other resources for teen writers.

These "commandments" may not end your development as a writer for teens, but they may represent an effective beginning. After all, it's one of the ironies of life that, for most of us, becoming an effective teen writer is a task that can easily require much of a lifetime. But that works out okay, because the enthusiasm of youth and the wisdom of the ages can make a potent combination when they are put together on paper.

All of which brings us to one last commandment, in closing:

10. Thou Shalt Never, Ever Useth Language Liketh This When Writingeth for Teens.

Endnotes

1. George Barna, *Generation Next (What You Need to Know About Today's Youth)* (Ventura, CA: Regal Books, 1995), p. 77.
2. Emily Costello, "It's All in the Details...," *Writer's Digest* (April 1996), p. 29.

Bob Hostetler is a writer, editor, and frequent speaker at churches, conferences, and retreats. He lives with his wife and two children in Hamilton, Ohio. His thirteen books, which include *They Call Me A.W.O.L.* and *Holy Moses (and Other Adventures in Vertical Living)*, have sold over three quarters of a million copies. He has coauthored seven books with Josh McDowell, including the best-selling *Right from Wrong (What You Need to Know to Help Youth Make Right Choices)* and *The New Tolerance*. Bob has twice received a Gold Medallion Book Award from the Evangelical Christian Publishers Association. He is also an Amy Award recipient.

16

How to Make a Living as a Freelance Writer

DR. DENNIS E. HENSLEY

To survive—yea, flourish—as a full-time freelance writer, you have to have a split personality.

—DENNIS E. HENSLEY

YOU ARE COMPLETELY OUT THERE on your own, so you are responsible for everything. By yourself. It's more than just wearing many hats; it's actually becoming many people.

As a freelance writer, I have no set salary coming in each week. (Set bills, yes; but salary, no!) I have no boss, editor, or publisher who expects me to arrive at an office at 8 a.m. I have no partners, no employees, no established customer base, and no paid holidays or vacations.

Some people envy the career I've had for the past twenty years, whereas others are terrified by it. All, however, are curious about it. In truth, very few people make a full-time living solely from freelance writing. Those of us who do have developed some very strict disciplines. Knowing about these disciplines can help you toward your goal of one day becoming a full-time writer.

NOT JUST THE CHAIRPERSON

After freelancing full-time for six years, I incorporated as a one-person corporation called Denehen, Incorporated (standing obviously, for DENnis E. HENsley). This move enabled me to deduct certain expenses—insurance, automobile, home office, computers—directly from my earnings. It also required that I pay corporate taxes, then pay separate taxes on my salary and bonuses and do a lot of paperwork for each level of government (city, county, state, and federal). As such, incorporation may or may not be something you eventually will want to explore for yourself.

The point, however, is that when I incorporated, the incorporation papers required that I establish a board of directors for my new company. For appearance sake, I listed my wife as Denehen's vice president; in reality, I was the whole show.

I think it was at that moment I realized how "on my own" I truly was. Other businesses had fifteen to thirty people on their boards who could advise the CEO on matters related to law, finance, taxes, public relations, advertising, and new product development. Not me. I was the whole board. (Yikes!)

What I finally decided to do was to go through the exercise of selecting a board of directors anyway. I asked myself, "If you were going to get regular advice from people on how best to make Denehen (i.e., yourself) work at peak efficiency, who would you hire?"

I got out a scratch pad and began to write down a list of advisors. I decided to hone it to ten. This is what I came up with: chairman, financial manager, business consultant, maintenance worker, arts and cultural docent, family counselor, assignments editor, fitness trainer, religious leader, and education mentor.

If you go through this exercise, remind yourself that, unlike a traditional company that has many employees, *you* will be the only worker. As such, you will need advice on both the business and personal levels. So devise your board accordingly.

From that point, I began to hold Monday morning board meetings with myself. I held myself accountable for progress in each of these ten crucial areas of my life, and each "board member" had to give a weekly report. Did each member always come with a success report? Not really. But when one didn't, he got a good talking to by the others and a stern warning to get back on track by the next meeting. Most of the time, he would (and still does).

Making It Work

Now, lest you think I'm reenacting a scene from *Sybil* or *Three Faces of Eve*, let me assure you that I don't literally talk to myself.

(Well, not in this situation anyway.) What I do is pull out my weekly diary and monthly calendar and begin to review what was supposed to have been accomplished and what actually did or didn't get done. My notes might run something like this:

Financial Manager

Deposited $x into corporate account this week from book royalties, magazine article sales, movie/audio/video/translation royalties, book doctoring, writers' conference lectures, etc. Spent $x on corporate expenses related to postage, phone bill, new equipment, transportation, subscriptions, research material, online service costs, quarterly estimated taxes, etc.

Analysis: Looking good. Income is running two to one over expenses, despite the purchase two months ago of a new computer system. One warning: A notice came from the corporation's hospitalization insurer saying rates will be increased by fifteen percent for the coming year. The budget needs to be adjusted accordingly.

Deposited $x into the family checking account as received from noncorporate related income (stock dividends, rental properties, mutual funds). Spent $x of family funds on household utilities, college tuition for son and daughter, family car upkeep, groceries, clothing, recreation, church and charities, haircuts, etc.

Analysis: Whoa! These college expenses are going through the roof—need to get the kids to check on scholarships or to increase their part-time work hours. One warning: Christmas shopping begins in two months, so money needs to be budgeted for that. In three months, the rental property leases need to be renewed. Check with tenants regarding whether they plan to stay another year and advise them of the new rent rate.

Business Consultant

Finished reading a book this week on concepts of investing in mutual funds. Made notes. When extra money comes in from royalties or advances, this could be a good place to invest so cash flow will come from a steady source during long periods between freelance checks. This week need to listen to a book on tape about leveraging real estate equity so as to keep money at peak velocity of earnings.

Maintenance Worker

Was supposed to take snow blower in for tune-up and call chimney sweep to clean out fireplace. Didn't do either due to time crunch. Need to put those items back on this week's schedule. Snow is coming soon. Need to be ready. Additionally, the car needs an oil change. Leave early for the fitness center one day and drive through one of those quick oil change places.

Arts and Cultural Docent

Was supposed to attend daughter's piano recital Tuesday (made it), wife's church choir presentation Wednesday night (made that too), and the charity function at the new wing of the art museum (missed that on purpose, just sent a check). Nothing special is set for this week, but it would be fun to take in a movie or at least rent a video one night. Reminder: The Andrew Lloyd Weber touring musical hits town in five weeks. Call for tickets now, or you won't get in.

Family Counselor

Called parents on Monday; sent Dad a birthday card on Wednesday; sent three e-mail messages to my sister this week, two to my brother. Took wife out to lunch on Tuesday. Spent time with whole family this week at meals, some TV, music events, church on Sunday. This week plan to go to video store with son one night (Thursday?), movie or video with wife, help daughter start looking for a car of her own.

Assignments Editor

Spent most of last week doing two major freelance magazine pieces and an afternoon doing research for chapter three of new book. This week I need to finish that third chapter of the book to stay on schedule. Also need to go through my in tray and pull notes for three query letters that need to go out. Need to deliver a guest lecture at the local writers' club on Wednesday at 7 p.m. (topic already chosen and outlined but notes need to be printed). Try to find time to reread and edit the short story that was rejected two weeks ago. (Editor sent suggestions for revisions.) Clean office, purge files of outdated material. Keep brainstorming about next book idea.

Fitness Trainer

Last week only managed to get to the fitness center two days due to pending deadlines on assignments, but managed to do some floor exercises and weight lifting at home. Need to try to get back to the club this week. Check weight (bring diet in line if showing any gain), use Nautilus™ equipment for muscle tone, use aerobic machines for heart conditioning.

Religious Leader

Attended church twice, plus men's Bible study on Saturday morning, personal devotions each day. Will be teaching a college and career Sunday school class next week, so need to get a lesson ready. How about something on Solomon and wisdom?

Education Mentor

Watched part three of that PBS special on World War I this past week. Read five chapters in Jack London's novel *Martin Eden*. Practiced the guitar a couple of times. Will continue this week with the PBS series, reading the novel, and pickin' the guitar. I'm content with these mental activities for the present.

Selecting Your Own Board

So it is that I am able to keep my life and my business in balance. I've shown this system to others, and they have used it successfully too. Most people alter the board members in ways that are most important to them. Some have such alter egos as a travel agent, wardrobe coordinator, gardener, gourmet cook, nanny, social director, library researcher, banker, publicity agent, booking agent, secretary, or housekeeper. Sometimes some board members are replaced by more needed ones.

Regardless of who comprises the board, it serves as a personal accountability team. It reminds you that independently employed people cannot concentrate all their energy in one area to the point of jeopardizing the success or continuance of other, equally vital areas.

So if you intend to strike out on your own someday, make sure that "your own" has enough depth and diversity to serve in the many different roles you will have to assume. Once you think you *are* at *that* level, pick up the gavel and call the meeting to order.

Dr. Dennis E. Hensley is an associate professor of English at the Fort Wayne campus of Taylor University, where he directs the creative writing program. His twenty-nine books include *Millennium Approaches* (Avon Books), *The Jesus Effect* (Pacific Press), *Writing for Profit* (Thomas Nelson), *The Freelance Writer's Handbook* (HarperCollins), *Write on Target* (The Writer), and the novel *The Gift* (Harvest House). He has written more than 3,000 newspaper and magazine articles and has served nine times as a judge for the annual Evangelical Press Association Awards. He is also a regional correspondent for *Writer's Digest* and a columnist and contributing editor for *Writer's Journal*, *Advanced Christian Writer*, and *The Christian Communicator*. You may reach him via e-mail at DNHensley@TaylorU.edu.

— 17 —

Book Proposals: Your Best Approach to Becoming a Published Author

STANLEY C. BALDWIN

Books aren't written—they're rewritten.
Including your own. It is one of the hardest things to accept,
especially after the seventh rewrite hasn't quite done it.
—MICHAEL CRICHTON

IT'S ALMOST EVERY WRITER'S dream to find someone actually willing to pay you for the privilege of publishing your book. But how do you make that dream a reality? That is the question. The answer is to learn early, before you even complete the manuscript, how to prepare a book proposal.

Perhaps you have already written a book manuscript. It's still true. If you want to find a publisher for your book, you need to learn how to create a winning book proposal. I define a book proposal as a "sampler package" that will give publishers a good idea of whether or not they want to publish your book.

You could, of course, simply send your completed book manuscript to every publisher for whom you can find an address. You could, but doing so would be a mistake.

Both your manuscript and you could perish from old age before you make the rounds of potential publishers. Not because publishers are that numerous, though there are hundreds of Christian publishers. Not because publishers are painfully slow in processing manuscripts, though some move at a near glacial pace. The primary reason that sending complete book manuscripts to publishers is ill-advised is that publishing ethics require you to submit to only one of them at a time. No such limitation applies to book proposals. You can, and I strongly urge that you do, submit to a number of publishers simultaneously.

To understand this situation, you need a glimpse inside the book publishing industry. Evaluating a promising book manuscript is a time-consuming and expensive process, usually involving a number of people from both the editorial and marketing divisions. Publishers don't want to spend a lot of time and money evaluating your manuscript only to discover that you have sold the manuscript elsewhere.

Proposals can be evaluated much quicker than complete manuscripts. The decision in response to a proposal is often less momentous as well. If the editor has the complete manuscript in hand, no mystery is left. It is either "go" or "no go." With a proposal, the editor can simply express interest and ask to see more before committing himself. With unpublished authors, that is probably what he will do.

Content of a Proposal

A book proposal has three elements, which should be arranged in this order: (1) a cover letter describing the book and author, (2) a table of contents or synopsis, and (3) sample chapters. Let's consider each of these elements.

Cover Letter

The cover letter is a short but vital element of your proposal. Short means it should take one page, two at the most. If two, do not fudge on margins; and pack in all the copy you possibly can. The idea is to be succinct, not to save paper.

Your cover letter should tell, first and foremost, what the book is about. I cannot overemphasize this point. You can hardly imagine how irritating it is to an editor to get a proposal that does not quickly come to the point and tell what the book is about.

Some proposals begin with everything else. They tell of the favorable responses of others to the material, or they cite someone prominent who commends it. Those are mistakes! As the editor, I may feel I am being manipulated. I don't really care when I look at your proposal who else says what. Let's hear your idea, and we'll see what I say about it.

Some authors tell first why they wrote the book or what their hopes are for it. That's not a good idea. Maybe such information belongs in this cover letter but not up front; right now I want to know what the book is about.

This means you must carefully craft a statement communicating the essence of your message. This theme statement must not be too broad, i.e., "This is a book about God's will for mankind." Still too broad is "God's will for the family" or "God's will for marriage."

"Learning to communicate with a noncommunicative spouse," is getting closer. Whatever theme you choose, stick with it. Don't wander off into some nearby meadow, no matter how inviting that territory seems and no matter what important things you have to say.

After you have clearly stated what your book is about, you may explain why you think the book is needed. Here you can include information about what is already on the market and how your book will be different.

However, don't confuse being different with being needed. They aren't the same thing. You may tell the editor quite correctly that no book on the market is like your treatise on Ezekiel's temple. To which the editor will probably respond, "And there is not about to be either."

Next include information about why you are qualified to write the book. Perhaps you have formal education in the subject. Or you have done extensive study on this topic. Or you have personal experience in this area.

Besides presenting your qualifications in the particular field for which you write, mention your publishing credits. If they are extensive, summarize or attach a separate sheet. Don't bog down the cover letter with tedious detail. If your credits are few or none, you may want to omit mentioning them; but the rest of your proposal had better sparkle.

Finally, tell the editor the approximate length of the book you envision (in words or pages or both), when you expect to deliver the complete manuscript, and whether this proposal is an exclusive or simultaneous submission.

You can do all this in less space than it has taken me to tell you about it. For example: "I expect the book to run about 200 pages. I can deliver it within six months of your go ahead. This is a simultaneous submission."

Table of Contents or Synopsis

If your book is nonfiction, send a table of contents. If it is fiction, send a synopsis (a condensed version) of the story.

Many works of fiction do not have chapter titles, and it won't mean much to an editor to read a table of contents listing the chapters as 1 through 30. Instead, give an overview of the story, taking from two to seven pages or more to indicate some of the complexity of the plot.

For nonfiction, your table of contents is more than a simple listing of chapter titles. With each title, you will include one to three paragraphs of description, showing how you will develop the chapter's theme.

This table of contents serves much the same purpose as an outline would, but it presents the material in the form that you will actually offer it. This is, after all, a book. It is not necessary to include both a table of contents and an outline. That risks wearying your busy editor or even confusing him.

Don't agonize over the table of contents as to the order of chapters or whether a given aspect of your subject will require one chapter or two. Your proposal is not like the Ten Commandments, established for all time and incapable of being altered. The table of contents simply shows the editor you have thought the presentation through, that it hangs together and make sense.

Sample Chapters

Include in your proposal some actual chapters from your book manuscript. Keep in mind that your sample chapters will reveal whether you can deliver the goods or not. Therefore, send in only polished and well-written chapters. How many? Two or three, depending on what the writers' guidelines request. Which ones? Probably the first and second, though you may send the first and last or some other selection that will make sense to the editor. If chapters are short and numerous, as they sometimes are in fiction and devotional books, you may want to send as many as ten.

COMMON QUESTIONS AND ANSWERS ABOUT PROPOSALS

Question: Should I send a proposal first, or should I precede it with a query letter asking if there's any interest?

Answer: You may send a query letter first. It is much like the cover letter described above without the table of contents and sample chapters. The advantage is that you need not send so much material and, in fact, do not even have to prepare it. The disadvantage is that an expression of interest by an editor won't mean much; and the next step will still be to provide a complete proposal. It adds a step to the process, and I rarely do it.

Question: To how many publishers should I send my proposal, and how do I select them?

Answer: Send your proposal to six or eight different publishers at a time. Actually, you can send to as many or as few as you please. I think six or eight is a practical number.

How to select them is a bit more difficult. I compile an A list and a B list. The A list contains the names of the publishers I most want to publish my book. They are the ones who receive my proposal first.

Selecting publishers for the A list is somewhat subjective. Choose those that:

Have a good record of publishing the type of book you want to write. If you send a "maverick" as some call it, meaning a product that does not fit the publisher's line with regard to length or genre, it will almost certainly be rejected.

Are well respected by their other authors.

Represent a good "fit" for you with regard to general theological and practical stance.

Obviously, you can only follow the above suggestions if you know something about the publishers. This may require some research at your Christian bookstore, in writers' market books, and at writers' conferences or critique groups.

Question: What kind of responses should I expect to my proposals?

Answer: Typically, if you send out eight good proposals, four or five may get timely declines (within two weeks to two months).

Two may get no response at all. One will stimulate an expression of some interest or a suggestion how it may be adapted or where it might best be marketed. One will sit indefinitely, leaving you to wonder whether to be hopeful about it or not. Of course, responses will vary; but these give some idea of what you might expect.

Question: What if more than one publisher responds affirmatively to my proposal?

Answer: Celebrate! But not too much. Affirmative responses are of two kinds.

1. "Looks interesting, please send us the complete manuscript." This response involves no commitment on the part of the publisher. However, if you are not previously published, it is about all you can expect. Reply immediately and tell the editor when you will deliver your manuscript. Express interest in any editorial input or suggestions. You might ask if the editor would be willing to evaluate your manuscript at the halfway point, assuming it's unwritten.
2. "We like it and want to publish it; a contract is enclosed (or will be coming soon)." You might even get a phone call to this effect.

Since you told the publisher in your cover letter that you were submitting simultaneously to others, you are perfectly free to continue dealing with more than one who has responded affirmatively. Just keep everything clear and above board. Don't tell one publisher the identity of the other(s), but do tell them others have expressed interest.

You may think that preparing a proposal involves a lot of work. Indeed it does. I estimate that for me it's about thirty to forty percent of the entire job. But that's better than completing a poorly planned manuscript that no one wants to publish. No one said getting a book published was going to be easy. But the satisfaction of a difficult job done well brings some of life's better moments.

STANLEY C. BALDWIN has authored twenty books, including four that have sold over 250,000 copies each. These include *Love, Acceptance and Forgiveness* with Jerry Cook (Regal), *The Kink and I* with Dr. James Mallory (Victor), *Your Money Matters* with Malcolm MacGregor (Bethany), and *What Did Jesus Say About That?* (Victor). Stan's books have been translated into eleven foreign languages. He is an ordained Baptist pastor and a former editor of *Power* take-home papers and Victor books. You may reach Stan by e-mail at SCBaldwin@juno.com. Let him know if you would like to receive the free International Christian Writers reports.

—— 18 ——

Contracts and Copyright Law

CECIL MURPHEY

If you would not be forgotten, as soon as you
are dead & rotten, either write things worth reading,
or do things worth the writing.

—BENJAMIN FRANKLIN

JENNIFER SKIPPED TO THE THIRD page of the contract and signed her name. "There," she said, folding it to send it back to the publisher.

"Aren't you going to read it?" I asked. "You may want to change something."

Like many writers who receive their first book contract, Jennifer's soft blue eyes stared incredulously at me. "We're all Christians, aren't we?"

I gave her a ten-minute overview of some bad contracts from CBA publishers. I wasn't trying to create problems. "This is business. Don't ever forget that, no matter who you deal with." I passed on two pieces of advice a much-published writer once gave me. "First, consider every contract a rough draft or a work in progress. Just because it's printed doesn't mean it can't be changed. Second, those who write contracts always give themselves the advantage."

My intention isn't to be contentious but to alert writers to items in book contracts they need to be aware of. Consider my advice as self-protection. Writers don't help themselves by trying to sound like Harvard-trained lawyers, but they do have the right to speak up for their own good.

Negotiating a Contract

In looking at a contract, think negotiation instead of compliance. Even though it may involve ministry, publishing is a business. Profit *is* the ultimate factor in offering contracts. So, in random order, here are the significant things to consider before you grab your pen to sign.

Option Clause

One of my favorite agents calls this the slave clause. It gives publishers the right to reject or buy your next book. Even in my most naive days, I crossed that out and initialed it. No publisher ever withdrew a contact because I refused their option.

Free Copies

Two decades ago, six was the standard number of free copies; now ten is common. Always ask for more. I co-wrote one book, and both of us received seventy-five simply because we asked. Some publishers are smart enough to know that writers give away many books as a promotional tool. But don't get greedy here. For example, I know one writer-speaker who refused to sign a contract because the publisher would give her only twenty-five free copies. When she insisted on a thousand books for promotion, they withdrew the contract. As far as I know, that book has never been published.

Advance and Royalty

Publishers have a standard advance policy ranging from zero to thousands of dollars. CBA publishers rarely offer six-figure advances. Think of it this way: The amount of the advance points to how well they expect the book to sell. Bigger advances imply more money budgeted for advertising and larger expected sales.

Although the royalty agreement seems fairly standard in the industry, at least for first-time book writers, ask for an "escalator" clause. After a book sells a certain number of copies, the royalty goes up. I had a work-for-hire contract that said after the book sold 70,000 copies, I would receive a thousand dollars for each thousand books sold.

Normally writers receive half the advance after signing (thirty days from the time the signed contract reaches the publishing house). The second half gets paid with the delivery of a "satisfactory manuscript." Most publishers don't pay the second half until they have completed the editing and some not until after publication.

I can think of two obvious reasons for delaying the second payment. First, the publisher wants to hold on to the money as long as possible. Second, some writers don't deliver what they promise in the proposal; or the final manuscript isn't acceptable to the publisher.

Occasionally writers refuse to make editorial changes. In frustration, publishers have returned manuscripts and canceled contracts. In such instances, unless they specifically state that the advance must be repaid, writers don't have to return it. "He might as well keep the money—it will be the last he'll ever get from us," said one exasperated editor.

Manuscript Acceptability

What happens if the publisher insists that the first half of the advance be repaid if they consider the final manuscript unacceptable, even after the author has made the requested revisions? No sensible writer would want to have such a clause included, but it may be something you can't change. At least be aware of it.

Publication of the Manuscript

Most contracts state that the house will publish your manuscript within a certain time, such as two years. You may want to negotiate for a shorter time frame, i.e., 18 months from the time the publisher receives the completed manuscript. Regardless of the time issue, insist that the rights revert to you if not published—without your having to pay back the advance.

Reversion Clause

Many books go out of print within a year after publication. If your career should take off five years from now, reprint rights can be invaluable to you. Some contracts state that after a certain number of years, such as five, the rights then revert to the author. Ask to have them revert as soon as the publisher declares the book out of print. If they don't agree, push for the rights reverting within a year or two.

Subsidiary Rights

Hold on to ancillary or multimedia rights. Four of my books, written before I had an agent, sold overseas because a foreign publisher read, liked, and wanted them. One book went out of print in 1985, and a Chinese house picked it up in 1993. Since then, each April I've received a small royalty check.

Retain the rights to audio cassette recordings of your work—a fast-growing area of popularity among a society of commuters. Above all, don't give away the rights to dramatic adaptation, especially movies or TV. Few writers will have their books made into smash Broadway hits or a TV mini-series, but who can tell?

Still vague and controversial, no one knows where electronic publishing is going, so retain those rights. If the publisher demands them, negotiate a limitation, such as an agreement for a separate advance and royalty. Make sure they're not part of the subsidiary rights split which is usually 50/50. If your publisher wants to create "derivative works in electronic form," resist signing those away. Today that means CD-ROMs; but in 2005, who knows what will be available? If you give up this right, you lose control over the final product.

Libel Clause

Most contracts have a clause similar to this: "The work does not contain any scandalous, libelous, or unlawful matter." That makes you responsible. Sometimes the contract states that the writer will hold the publisher harmless against all claims. This is standard.

Don't, however, underestimate the wrath of your friends, even if you say nice things about them. If you use their names in nonfiction, publishers insist that they sign a statement giving permission for any material that relates to them. In 1997, Servant sent me a form for everyone mentioned in my book. "They sign, or you change their names," came the instructions.

The Most Important Clause

Don't sign any contract unless it states something like this: "Any rights not expressly granted herein to the Publisher reside exclusively with the Author."

COPYRIGHTS, FAIR USE, AND PERMISSIONS

So you're afraid publishers will steal your idea? You worry that they'll offer your proposal to another writer and cut you out?

If you're really worried, this section probably won't help. Here's why. (1) Publishers committed to theft will steal your idea but disguise it enough that no court can convict them. (2) Ideas are everywhere. A friend once said, "Every day, God stands above the universe and throws down five new ideas. Those who are attuned, grab the ideas first." It's quite possible that others do have similar ideas for an article or a book.

So far as I know, no one has ever stolen any of my work, and I've been publishing for more than twenty-five years. I've heard a few horror stories, but they involved screenplays and Hollywood. There's probably no way to protect yourself from the unscrupulous, especially if they rejected your proposal and if it wasn't a completed product. Even so, you need to know the basics of copyright law.

Here are the essentials for writers to understand about copyright. Consult a lawyer who specializes in copyright law if you have questions.

Copyright is a form of protection provided by the laws of the United States to the authors of "original works of authorship." The protection covers published and unpublished works.

If you sell your manuscript to a publisher, your copyright is registered as part of the contract. If you want to register your own copyright or have questions, contact the Copyright Office. They don't give legal advice, but they do have forms and circulars available. For information, call 202-707-3000. If you want forms, pamphlets, or circulars, call the forms hot line at 202-707-9100 or fax at 202-707-2600. You may write to: Copyright Office, Library of Congress, Washington, DC 20559-6000, or you can download forms on the Internet at www.loc.gov/copyyright.

You can't copyright an idea, title, plot, fact, or news.

As soon as you finish writing anything, you are protected by "common law copyright."

"A common misconception is that you must register a work with the U.S. Copyright Office for it to be protected by copyright. Under present law, copyright exists *automatically* from the moment a work is fixed in a tangible medium of expression. Therefore, registration with the Copyright Office is not necessary."[1]

If you own a copyright on a work, you have the right to make other versions of it, turn it into another literary form, deliver, read, or present it in public for profit. Your creation belongs to you. If anyone copies, excerpts, adapts, or publishes your material without permission, that person has violated your rights.

If you think others have violated your copyright, you have to prove two facts: (1) substantial similarity between the two works and (2) evidence that the infringers took your protected expression and used it as their own.

The present copyright law says that works created after January 1, 1978, are yours for your lifetime plus seventy years. Anything written before 1978 had a copyright of twenty-eight years plus a renewal for another forty-seven, for a total of seventy-five years. After that the work went into public domain—most of the time.

Public domain applies only to the original works. If someone has revised or updated the work, you can't count the revision as being in public domain. For instance, Victor Hugo wrote *Les Miserables* nearly 200 years ago and in French. That work is clearly in public domain. But if you quote from an English translation or a condensation, it may be under copyright. For example, I have a 1961 condensed English version owned by CBS. Check the copyright date on anything you quote. If you're unsure about a copyright expiration, contact the Copyright Office by mail or on the Internet.

Quoting from copyrighted material is where copyright trouble arises. If you want to quote from a published source, how much of it can you use without permission? Answer: No one really knows. We talk about "fair use" which means a reasonable amount. One lawyer called the idea of fair use the "most troublesome in the copyright world." So how much is fair? Some publishers allow 250 words, others 500. Most members of the American University Press Association permit 1,000, providing you give credit. This rule excludes song lyrics, letters, poems, short stories, and essays that are complete units. If you're not sure, query the copyright holder. If you do quote a reasonable amount, always give credit. But never use more of a copyrighted work than is necessary to make your point. The more you borrow, the more you face the charge of unfair use.

Lawyers argue more over how writers use copyrighted material than the amount. Think of it this way: If you're reviewing or critiquing, you can quote freely from the material. If you're citing a competitive work, you need to contact the publisher for permission.

If you are going beyond fair use and you want to quote from copyrighted material, you need to obtain permission from the copyright owner. You can usually get the information from the copyright page of a book. Simply write to the owner of the copyright and ask permission. I've always sent a copy of the general context that includes the quotation. Explain how you plan to use the material and who will publish it.

If the owner wants payment for such usage, you're the one who pays unless your publisher agrees to do so or to split the cost. (This payment may be a factor in the contract negotiation.)

So either pay or don't quote. You can paraphrase it; but a lawyer friend said that if the paraphrase is too close to the original, it could be counted as unfair use and a violation of copyright.

If you write a work-for-hire manuscript, the publisher usually owns the material. That means you are writing something that is "specially ordered or commissioned" by a publisher. The contract, signed by both parties, must state that it is a work for hire. Once the book is out of print, you can ask the publishers to turn the copyright and reprint rights over to you. At present, I have rights to nineteen work-for-hire books previously published by Fleming H. Revell.

Copyright laws are already complex. Now that electronic rights have come on the scene, the laws are still evolving. If you have questions, get answers before you inadvertently infringe on a copyright.

ENDNOTE

1. Lloyd J. Jassin and Steven C. Schechter, *The Copyright Permission and Libel Handbook* (New York: John Wiley, 1998), p.12.

Cecil Murphey is the author of fifteen fiction books, fifty-one nonfiction books, and over five hundred articles. He has been a two-time finalist for the Gold Medallion Book Awards as well as a 1996 winner for *Rebel with a Cause*, the autobiography of Franklin Graham. He is also an ordained Presbyterian minister and was a missionary with Elim Fellowship, Kenya, East Africa from 1961-1967. Cec has taught at more than 125 writers' conferences as well as at six colleges. Some of his best known books are *Gifted Hands*, the story of Ben Carson M.D. (Zondervan); *Think Big*, also with Dr. Carson; and *Invading the Privacy of God* (Servant).

— 19 —

Working with Agents

CECIL MURPHEY

Books are never finished—they are merely abandoned.
—OSCAR WILDE

"HOW DO I GET AN AGENT?" is the most common question I hear. Smart writers ask it when they know the answer to two prior questions.

WHY WOULD AN AGENT WANT ME FOR A CLIENT?

The first question to ask is: "Why would an agent want me for a client?" Reputable agents stay busy selling. That's their job, and they make their income by commission. Even so, most agents—even the busiest—are open to queries. They want to find writers they can enthusiastically represent and eagerly seek the next great, prolific writer whose books will top the best-seller lists.

Too many writers obsess over the idea that they aren't "real" writers until they have an agent. In Christian publishing, most publishers are still open to writers without agents. Even in the American Booksellers Association (ABA), small publishers and regional houses still read unagented books. Too many writers don't believe these facts. They must have an agent, so they do the most obvious thing: They read a myriad of articles in *Writer's Digest* or a book guaranteed to tell them how to land an agent. They're the ones who write the query letters that, by following the guidelines exactly, will be irresistible. A few of them bypass the query and shoot off a proposal, convinced an agent is sitting at her desk, waiting and dreaming of such a proposal to come in. Sometimes those attempts to get represented actually pay off. But they are the miracles of publishing, almost like winning a lottery without buying a ticket.

With a little preparation, writers can increase their chances of being represented. It's easier to sign with an agent when they ask, "Why would an agent want me for a client?" Most writers know what they want to sell, but they may not always know what an agent wants to handle. They'll do better if they ask, "What can I do to meet an agent's needs?" Here are five items that point to those needs.

Knowledge of the Agent's Specialty

Most literary agencies—especially the smaller ones—specialize. Some handle nonfiction exclusively, or perhaps they do eighty percent nonfiction. Others specialize in genre fiction, and writers who want agents had better figure out what that means. Some agents work exclusively with the Christian Booksellers Association (CBA). I know of one Christian agent whose focus is to get Christian writers into the ABA, and she's good at what she does.

So how do writers learn the agent's special emphasis? Here are three easy ways to figure that out. Go to the library, and consult the annual publication *Literary Market Place* which is industry wide. In the *Christian Writers' Market Guide*, Sally Stuart states what Christian agents handle. The third way is to search the Internet; agents are now displaying Web pages. They list what they handle and often their recent sales. One New York agent holds a chat session every two weeks.

When writers figure out the agent whose focus represents what they have to sell, doesn't that give them a better chance for success?

Publishing Credits

Second, agents like clients with publishing credits. Credits mean articles and stories—anything in print. A number of writers have turned to agents when they have a contract offered and use that fact as an enticement. If writers show they're persistent, that they're learning the craft and getting published—even in small magazines—they're more apt to get their manuscripts looked at than if they write, "This is the first thing I've ever written."

Productivity

Third, productive writers interest agents. After all, they make their livelihoods from selling, and they can only sell the books their clients produce. When someone plans to write only one book (usually an autobiography) and the agent also gets a query from someone who has four manuscript proposals, guess who has the edge?

One agent said, "An author who is currently publishing is always most exciting. After all, I know I'll have the opportunity to jump in and begin negotiating something that's already rolling. I also know that author's work sells. I can then position the author for better deals and wider exposure."

Professionalism

Fourth, agents seek professional clients. When I asked one agent about new authors, she said, "I put a high priority on attitude. Is that person respectful in dealing with me? Is she someone who knows she needs her work edited and reedited? Or is she someone who thinks she'll be able to treat me like an employee and that she's written *War and Peace* in a single draft?"

For example, an agent who had previously worked with a large publishing house received a phone call from a writer who sought representation. The woman started by mentioning a man's name and said, "He worked for them, too, and he's never heard of you. So are you a real agent?"

The agent was ready to slam down the phone, but he patiently said, "That house has been hiring editors for eighty years; and a lot of talent came and went." Then he added, "I never heard of your friend either. Does that mean he didn't edit for them?" I won't bother to tell you whether the agent agreed to represent that discourteous writer.

Professional attitude—whether previously published or not—is of utmost importance. Another agent referred to the "community" of the Romance Writers of America. She said they had about

6,000 members, of whom 1,500 have been published. After she had attended several conferences, she said, "Everyone I met behaved like a total professional. They understood what an agent does and how to approach one politely. They understood the importance of hard work. Those are things that mean a lot to me in making my decisions of whom to represent."

Platform for Promotion

Fifth, of course, is marketability. If an author has a great nonfiction work but no appropriate avenue for promoting the work—no platform or ministry—that makes it a tough sell in the CBA market. By contrast, in fiction, marketability can actually mean: Does it stick to the conventions? Although everyone wants a fresh concept, in genre fiction, publishers (and agents) want it to abide by readers' expectations. "If I get a romance submission set in Greece, I'd have to be wary because that setting is a tough sell."

Once writers determine why an agent might want them, the next big question to ask is: "Do I really need an agent?"

Do I Really Need an Agent?

Too many writers get caught up in what I call the "writing mystique." They begin as aspiring writers and think that to progress as writers they must have an agent so they can become "real writers."

There used to be one definition of a writer—a person who had published. Now it's been extended: One who has published and has an agent. If an author doesn't have agent representation, he or she obviously has not become a Real Writer.

Maybe it's the glamour surrounding the word *agent*. Possibly we professionals have unintentionally misled those at the starting gate. We've worked too hard at impressing beginners with our achievements. After all, most of us know the spotlight focuses on us if we start a sentence with, "My agent said...." Perhaps we who have agents need to set things right by asking inquirers, "Why do you need an agent?" Or—and this is riskier—"Why do you think you're ready for an agent?"

Few writers want to hear such questions. Too many like to believe they have completed a manuscript to make an agent salivate—if only they could get an agent to read it. For instance, one man called me and begged me to recommend him to my agent. After I had asked him the third time, "Why do you think you're ready for an agent?" he said, "Because I've had all my manuscripts rejected." He hurriedly explained that his work was good—he knew it was—and if he could get an agent, the books would sell and bring in big advances.

"Has it occurred to you," I asked, "there is a reason you keep getting rejected? Perhaps your work may not be polished or focused enough or—?" That was as far as I got. He knew he could write, and he didn't need any help there. He wanted help in selling. He hung up angry.

Before writers obsess over getting an agent, they need to try the old method of proving themselves—or earning the right to be represented by an agent. Most of the successful writers I associate with started by writing and selling articles or short stories. They learned to slant for *The Upper Room* or *Discipleship Journal* or to draft stories for Sunday school take-home papers. In short, they learned the craft first. Okay, so once every fifty years, someone who has written his or her first novel signs a contract for a 3.7 million dollar advance. Sure it happens, but not to anyone I know. Besides, I don't like the odds.

My Story

I'll share how I did it, which isn't much different from most of my writer friends. I've earned my living as a writer since 1984, but I began selling in 1971. During those years, I sold a dozen books and more than 400 articles. Even then, I wasn't ready for an agent. Finally, in 1990, I was ready and signed with an agent who was excited about representing me.

Go back and reread the middle of the previous sentence: "I was ready." Those are the key words. I had already learned the business end of writing; I had improved my techniques as a writer. I had written manuscripts, mailed them out, screamed with delight over acceptance checks, and groaned over rejection slips. In the process, I learned to polish my material and developed a feel for what was marketable. When I signed with an agent, I was ready.

For years, I was writing and selling most of what I wrote. Then something happened. It was like having my own expanding business, and I wanted to focus my energy and time on what I did best—write. I could hire someone to do what I did less well—market. I didn't want an agent because I couldn't sell; I wanted one because I was already selling. An agent took that part of the work and freed me to concentrate on creating manuscripts. I was willing to pay for those services.

Factors to Consider

Some writers don't need agents. They have a gift for selling, so why should they give up fifteen percent to hire someone to do what they can do remarkably well? Writers need agents when they're selling regularly, when they show they are committed to the business of writing. And it is a business. It may be ministry or a cause, but it's a business first.

Most agents are willing to take on new clients, but they want writers whose work they can sell. If they sign up enough of them, they earn a good living. That's called business. Publishers want to discover new authors but authors whose work they can sell to the public and make a profit for the publishing house. That's also called business.

Now comes the real question most writers want answered: "How do I sign a contract?"

How Do I Sign a Contract for an Agent to Represent Me?

"Sign with any agent who'll take you as a client." That's good advice in three instances I can think of. One, if a writer is still living in a time warp before 1990 when few reputable agents agreed to represent Christian writers. Two, if a writer needs an agent more than an agent needs him. That is, if he can't sell any of his nine manuscripts and he thinks the agent can work magic. Three, if a writer has little confidence in her writing ability. She's so excited that if any agent is interested, her first question becomes, "Where do I sign?"

The agent-writer game has changed in the past decade. More agents are now setting up offices. I remember when the listing of agents in Sally Stuart's *Christian Writers' Market Guide* barely filled a single page. Her 1998 edition has six pages, and new names appear in her monthly updates because more Christian agents are looking for clients.

The ABA has come alive to the reality that Christians actually read. More than that, they buy books—lots of books. Not only are ABA publishers smiling at us, but previously uninterested agents are now beginning to salivate over the possibilities.

Given the reality of the shifting times, here's my advice before a writer signs with an agent.

Look at Listings of Agents

Sally Stuart's book is a good starting place. Also try the *Literary Market Place* at the library, and check the Internet. Ask your friends about agents. Even if they don't have an agent, they may have had contact with a few or know of others. If you're already publishing books, ask an editor, "What agents do you like to work with the most?" I know one agent who sells because he represents several well-known names, but the buzz is that many editors dislike him immensely. I suspect he doesn't do well with new writers.

Check Out the Agents

Before you make contact with agents, find out what you can about them. Why not call the Better Business Bureau in their city although they will tell you only if they've had complaints. If they have, won't that guide your thinking? Make sure you know what kind of manuscripts an agent represents. The annual *Guide to Literary Agents* gives a percentage of nonfiction and fiction. If you write fiction, you'll probably want to avoid someone whose agency handles eighty percent nonfiction.

Contact Several Agents

Send agents a one-page query letter that includes a paragraph about the project and one about you. Pitch only one project. When you query, think of it as your personal sales pitch. If you can't sell yourself, ask a friend to help; or pay someone to help you send a first-class "ad" about yourself.

Ask Questions

When agents respond, ask such questions as, "What books have you placed recently and with whom?" One agent I checked out on the Internet listed four "recent" sales—and the latest was dated 1996. Three of them were with small publishers. Be sure to ask, "Whom do you represent? Would you give me a few names and permission to ask them for a reference?" A few weeks ago, my agent asked permission to give my name to inquirers. After I consented, two writers contacted me by e-mail to ask about her.

You may also want to ask, "How long have you been in business?" Some writers believe new agents are hungrier. Others say they want experience. Be sure to ask, "How many clients do you handle? How large is your staff?" Some people like working with a large agency. Others, like me, believe we get more personal attention from a one-agent office.

Especially Look at the Money

Agents make a commission on their sales, usually fifteen percent. That's the total source of their income, so watch for add-on charges. Does your prospective agent charge a reading fee? You'll have to make up your mind about that. My advice? Pass that one by. When agents agree to look at manuscripts, they don't need to read one hundred pages before they make up their minds. Most of them decide within the first two or three pages.

Other charges include telephone and mailings. That's fairly common practice. Recently I've begun to hear of "retainer fees" by agents. One writer friend sent $150 a month retainer fee to a apparently reputable New York agent. His reasoning was that it would nudge the agent. After a year, my friend stopped sending money. He never got a sale and never received any accounting of the places the agent sent the manuscript.

Whatever you do, don't take the advice of an agent that says, "If you'll work with an editorial service, such as Perfect Grammar, I'll look at your material again." This scam seems too obvious to explain. However, if half a dozen agents read your work and turn it down, you may want to contact a bona fide editorial or critique service before you contact another agent.

Meet the Agent in Person

Not everyone needs to meet an agent in person, but doing so was essential for me. I was with my previous agency for six years;

and when I changed, I knew the kind of person I wanted to represent me. In 1997, I met face to face with two agents and would have met with a third one except I had found the one I wanted.

Because of the kind of person I am, I need an agent who will let me pitch ideas and give me feedback, one who doesn't mind being contacted once or twice a month about possible projects. Too many agents respond with, "Send me a proposal," or "Give me a one-page summary, and then we'll talk." I get a lot of ideas, and one out of every twenty-seven is good. My current agent will listen to all twenty-seven.

Also, I wanted an agent who would tell me why publishers turned me down. My current agent recently faxed me copies of letters from six top ABA houses that said no. Even though I didn't like the results, it was one more way my agent assured me she was doing her best for me.

End the Contract

This point may sound like preparing for a divorce before you have the wedding, but don't think of a relationship with an agent as a lifelong commitment. Most of my agented friends have switched at least once. Sometimes a writer outgrows the vision of the agent and wants to move into new fields. Or the agency may say, "We haven't sold anything of yours for eighteen months, so we're going to part company."

Most agents offer a one-year contract to new clients. If the agent sells within a year, the relationship goes on until one party wants out. The contract usually says that either party must send a letter sixty days in advance. It's that simple.

FINAL TIPS

In dealing with agents, be professional—this is business. Be courteous—you're dealing with human beings. I didn't make any suggestions about praying, but I assume you don't need any prompting there.

When writers meet the qualifications agents are looking for and decide why they need an agent, the chances are much, much better that an agent will say, "I'd love to represent you."

Cecil Murphey is the author of fifteen fiction books, fifty-one nonfiction books, and over five hundred articles. He has been a two-time finalist for the Gold Medallion Book Awards as well as a 1996 winner for *Rebel with a Cause*, the autobiography of Franklin Graham. He is also an ordained Presbyterian minister and was a missionary with Elim Fellowship, Kenya, East Africa from 1961-1967. Cec has taught at more than 125 writers' conferences as well as at six colleges. Some of his best known books are *Gifted Hands*, the story of Ben Carson M.D. (Zondervan); *Think Big*, also with Dr. Carson; and *Invading the Privacy of God* (Servant).

—— 20 ——

Gift Books: A Whole Different Animal

Gwen Ellis

Art is the manipulation of
someone else's imagination.
—Sol Saks

Writing gift books is comprised of components of both good news and bad news. The good news is that more gift books are being produced in the Christian market; they are beautiful and are meeting needs. Plus they don't take a lot of time to write. And they are fun to do.

The bad news is that because design costs are so high, publishers cannot pay large advances and royalties. They are more willing to hire compilers to do the job than to pay authors to do something publishers can do themselves, but few writers are willing to become compilers and not have their names listed as author.

With this good news/bad news firmly in mind, let's get serious about the making of gift books. Not long ago, I went through a serious illness that kept me incapacitated for a number of months. Over the course of the illness, I received at least two hundred greeting cards. Every card blessed my soul and meant much to me, but after I had moved them for the second or third time when changing homes, I decided to part with them. During that illness, I also received two or three gift books. I still have them, and I turn to them from time to time for encouragement and strength. A gift book has a lasting quality.

A gift book—a lasting gift—offers more inspiration than greeting cards for only a dollar or two more than a card costs. On a recent foray to a card store, I purchased several cards. When I totaled the cost, I discovered those cards averaged $3.50 each. But you can purchase a gift book for around $5.00. Those who receive gift books will probably keep them for a long time to mull over the thoughts and Scripture again and again. And gift books often are passed on to others.

Gift Books Require Thought

When I became Gift Product Director at Zondervan, I found I had to step into a whole new mind-set. Gift books are not how-to books. Gift books are not issue-oriented. Gift books are not novels. They contain no overt teaching directed at the purchaser of the book. The need for gift books is the need to have the right gift for a friend who is ill or having a birthday. They are for special occasions like Mother's and Father's Day. They are for Christmas gifts and Easter presents. They are stocking stuffers and basket fillers. For me, they are a whole new paradigm.

When I was being interviewed for my job, I became excited about the prospect of getting God's Word into the hands of those who receive gift books. I was excited because inspirational books cross into the general market easily and minister to those who buy them. I saw gift books as a way to get God's Word into the hands and hearts of people who would never darken the door of a church, never shop in a Christian bookstore, and never open a Bible.

In a lovely format, a gift book includes choice nuggets from Scripture to encourage hearts and perhaps even guide readers toward Christ. So while Christian gift books may look like pieces of fluff, the truth is they pack a powerful wallop of God's Word—dynamite in a pretty package.

Gift Books Fit Special Occasions

Let's take a look at the market. What are the occasions for giving gift books?

Christmas

The biggest gift-giving occasion of the year is Christmas. We remember the birthday of our Lord by giving gifts to each other. Moms give gift books to kids, teens, parents, and husbands. Dads give gift books to parents, kids, and especially to their wives. Single people give beautiful gift books to each other. Children look for cute, inexpensive gift books to give parents and grandparents. Grandparents give gift books to everybody.

Gift books become stocking stuffers, add-ons to a larger gift, pre-Christmas gifts, hostess gifts, and tokens of thanks. They are the perfect "little something" to give to close family members or those who offer service to you throughout the year.

Valentine's Day

This is the day of love, so gift books released for Valentine's Day are usually for couples or engaged people to give one another. Of course, the books focus on the subject of love, commitment, and God's perfect love for us. Not many publishers can release gift books solely for Valentine's Day, however. So in planning books to be released in time for this occasion, publishers also think about how the book can be used as a shower gift, wedding gift, and for the multitude of people who celebrate wedding anniversaries every June.

Easter

Of all the holidays, this is the one Christians should look forward to celebrating the most. Christianity was born on the first Easter when our resurrected Lord walked out of his tomb and gave us the hope of eternal life. This event is what separates us from Muslims, Buddhists, and people of other religions who worship at their leaders' tombs. We serve a risen Lord and an empty tomb. His resurrection is worthy of great celebration—and great gift books.

In recent years, some gift book companies have released wonderful books pointing us to the true meaning of Easter. These books remind us of the Lord of Easter and point us toward the Cross. They reveal the message found in the meaning of Jesus' names.

Those who give Easter books are those who want to focus attention on the Christ of the Cross. These books are also purchased as gifts for friends, family members, pastors, and other church leaders.

Wedding and Anniversaries

Most people have little time to talk with a bride and groom at a wedding. They pass rather quickly through a receiving line and have only a moment to express a thought to the couple; it never seems like enough time. A gift book can be the answer to that dilemma. A beautiful gift book will deliver the deepest message of your heart to the new pair. It can also give them a scriptural basis for their marriage and lives. A well-thought-out bridal and/or anniversary gift book can be a wonderful blessing in the lives of couples.

Memorial Day

A small book of remembrances can be a comfort on this holiday to those who look back on the loss of someone. Books that speak comfort, encouragement, hope, and gratitude for service rendered their country are appropriate for gift giving at this time. Publishers have not made special books for this holiday, but many of the books for other occasions are suitable.

Grandparents' Day

This is a new holiday that falls in the middle of September. Many publishers have not yet begun to make books specifically for it. However, the event seems to be growing in popularity, and if there are to be gift books for grandparents, this would be the prime time to release them.

Grandparents play an important part in our culture and in the lives of their grandchildren. The whole idea of passing on the faith needs to be developed and encouraged, and a pleasant way to do so would be through an appreciation gift book for grandparents.

Thanksgiving Day

Any gift book constructed for Thanksgiving Day needs to have a broader focus about giving thanks—gratitude—in general. Thanksgiving has been swallowed by Christmas preparations. It's too bad because an attitude of gratitude is a healing and healthy attitude for all of us to develop. So a gift book that could be used any time of year to help us express our gratitude is be a good idea. Such a book could then be released for Thanksgiving and have its prime promotion then.

GIFT BOOKS ARE NOT EASY TO WRITE

Gift books look easy to write because they are short and have more visual elements than other kinds of writing. But because they are short they must be thought out carefully. Every word must work and count for something significant. Gift books are a combination of nuggets mined from your own experience, quotations from others, and Scripture—all perfectly blended to create a whole image—an emotional response, a feeling.

Publishers are looking for new ideas for gift books. Some of those will come from their own publishing teams, some from printers with new techniques, many from research and observation, and some from idea people like yourself. Gift book producers visit gift markets and shows, super–sized bookstores, craft shops, and gift stores searching for fresh ideas.

Your ideas may be just what a publisher is looking for, but be aware that they will need to be unique. That means you'll have to visit all the same places they do, and then think and think and think. The next best idea is just waiting to be discovered. And you might be the person to discover it.

Some publishers require that permissions be obtained for all quoted material, some just for longer quotes, and some ask for no permissions at all as long as the length of the quote is within copyright law. Find out what your publisher will need with the completed project. It may turn out to be your job to obtain permissions for the material you quote, so keep careful records of the sources of your quotes as you compile the book.

GIFT BOOKS ARE COSTLY

Full-color printing is expensive. So are gilt edges, ribbon markers, padded covers, embossing, and gold foil. If you put them all in one book, it will be expensive to print for sure. But that's what gift books are about—a look, a feel.

Because they are costly to produce and are sold at high discounts, publishers cannot offer a high percentage royalty. Often there will be little or no royalty. Some publishers feel that unless your name adds real value to the product, they would rather hire a freelancer to compile the text and pay a substantial fee rather than have a royalty arrangement. As I said at the beginning of this chapter, there's good news/bad news here. The bad news about royalties I've already told you. Now let's talk about the good news.

WRITING A GIFT BOOK

It's important to know what your goals are when compiling gift books. Are you trying to establish a name for yourself as an author? Are you interested in the income? Are you hoping to hit it big in both areas?

Time for some realism. The only gift book I can think of that brought lasting fame to an author is Anne Morrow Lindberg's *Gift from the Sea,* although there may be others. So if you want to become known as a great writer, choose another genre.

Do you want to make a lot of money? The royalty arrangement needed to make the book financially feasible will preclude your getting rich. Even if a lot of books are sold, the monetary return to the author will be small.

A better plan may be to become a compiler of gift books—a compiler who is known for careful workmanship and lots of great ideas. You will receive a one-time payment and a byline somewhere in the book, but not necessarily on the cover. You will be paid as soon as the project is finished, and you can go on to the next project. In addition to being paid up front, you may be able to negotiate the purchase of books at a discount so you can sell them when you speak or teach.

Most publishers do not have enough staff to fill the need for compiling gift books in house. Even if they did, their gift books would eventually all begin to look and sound alike. So publishers reach far and wide through a network of freelancers for fresh perspectives.

Here's your opportunity. Publishers are looking for people to help compile gift books, and you may be just who they are looking for. So get a résumé and a few writing samples together and start contacting publishing houses, offering your services as a compiler.

Publishers tend to do gift books in series. They may do a series of "simple thoughts." They may be looking for material for each member of the family's birthday. They may be searching for fresh ideas for Christmas, Mother's or Father's Day, or any other holiday. Offer a series idea.

Keep in mind that the ideas you generate need to meet the widest segment of the population possible. For example, a Mother's Day book will be more successful if it is geared to mothers of all ages and not just the narrower segment of mothers of toddlers. The latter may be a valid idea, but the publisher will be interested in selling the book to the broadest group of mothers possible. A book for women needs to include material appropriate for single women and the issues they face as well as married women.

Think of the gift-giving occasions listed previously. Think of relational books. Think of a great story that could be turned into a gift book. Think of a classic that deserves to be brought back to life as a gift book. Think of favorite books of yours and how they could be reformatted as gift books. Think about times when you wanted to give a certain kind of gift book and couldn't find it. Think of a time when a gift book ministered to your need and make one like it.

You don't have to reinvent the wheel when it comes to gift books. Go to bookstores or gift shops and see what the secular press is doing. Go to card shops and look at designs and sentiments. Copy the basic idea and add Scripture and a Christian perspective to it. Get a stock photo book, and page through it. Think about ways the photos could be pulled into a theme book with appropriate text. Read your Bible, meditate on the meaning of Scripture passages, and think how you could help a publisher visualize them so more people can and will enjoy God's Word.

And then create a gift that will last.

GWEN ELLIS is currently Director of Gift Product at Zondervan Publishing House. She has written nine books, including three gift books.

Her latest releases are *Decorating on a Shoestring* co-authored with Jo Ann Janssen (Broadman & Holman), *By His Pattern: A Devotional for Needlework Lovers* (Tyndale), and *101 Ways to Make Money at Home* (Vine). Gwen has a new book coming from Baker Book House later this year. She is the mother of two grown children and lives with two black-and-white cats named Charles Dickens and Tiny Tim.

— 21 —

Writing the Romance Novel

CAROLE GIFT PAGE

The first thing you have to consider when writing a novel is your story, and then your story—and then your story!

—FORD MADOX FORD

David…took [Rachel's] hand in his…. "Sweetheart, I've been so worried about you. It's Christmas and I hate this animosity between us. Isn't there something we can do to resolve this?"…

Tears gathered behind Rachel's eyes. She yearned to collapse into David's arms and pretend these bitter weeks apart had never happened, that this was like every other Christmas they had spent together.[1]

This is the stuff of romance novels. No matter the setting, theme, or plot of your story, the focus is on the exciting, heart-stirring, unpredictable relationship between a man and a woman. And for the inspirational romance, the relationship is a triangle—a man, a woman, and God.

CHARACTERISTICS OF INSPIRATIONAL ROMANCE

The romance novel is much like the mainstream novel, with some notable exceptions.

Length and Complexity

The romance novel is usually shorter (70,000 words or less), much narrower in scope, and lighter in subject matter. Subplots must enhance the romance and not overshadow it. Your Romeo and Juliet must remain on center stage throughout the book; it's their story. Be prepared to give them a rocky, heart-wrenching, emotion-filled, tummy-tickling roller-coaster ride, complete with a happy ending.

Emotion

Emotion is everything. So is conflict. Editor Anne Canadeo of Steeple Hill stresses the importance of a "strong romance track," of portraying a couple's relationship with deep "emotional texture" and a significant conflict that threatens their love and eventually makes it stronger.

Family Values

Family values are in. Editors love stories that involve weddings, children, and babies. Both hero and heroine should be admirable, likable, intelligent people with strong family and community ties. In other words, create characters your readers can identify with. Forget the lustful scoundrel of some secular romances. Readers want a tender, sensitive hero with a strong character, worthy motives, and lofty goals. And, of course, he should be marvelously handsome and larger than life!

Love Scenes

Nix the love scenes. In the inspirational romance, your couple must remain chaste, saving themselves for marriage. While the attraction between hero and heroine should be unmistakable, descriptions of physical closeness must be handled discreetly. If you're not certain how much is too much, read a few inspirational romances to see how intimacy and sexual tension is handled.

Spiritual Values

Inspirational romances focus not only on a couple finding each other but also finding God or growing in their relationship with Christ. The potential for ministry in such romances is unlimited—and exciting!

In the "Dear Reader" letter at the end of my novel *In Search of Her Own*, I wrote:

> I love writing romances about people of faith, because it gives me a chance to explore the ideal romance—not just two people deeply in love, but God's boundless love for his people who've strayed from his side. God knew we could never be strong enough to find our way back to him, so he came to us in the person of his Son. Jesus, the most romantic figure in history, left the glory of heaven to take the form of a man so he could bear our sorrows and pay the price for our sins. He expressed the ultimate love, laying down his life for us and offering eternal fellowship with him. No wonder Scriptures refer to Christ as the Groom and his rescued people as his Bride. We are his beloved, his pearl of great price. And what does Jesus ask in return? Only that we accept him and love him with all our hearts.[2]

See what I mean? The romance novel offers a wonderful platform for introducing readers to the Lover of their souls. Now let's look at the ten steps I take when I sit down to write a romance novel.

STEPS FOR WRITING ROMANCE FICTION

1. *Begin with an Idea for a Particular Theme, Plot, or Character; and Weave All Three Together*

Theme is the essential message that holds the action together the way an invisible thread holds together a pearl necklace. It's your "takeaway," the central impression you want to leave with your reader. It gives organization, direction, and unity without calling undue attention to itself. Theme is what plot and characters are strung on.

Writing your romance without a clear-cut theme is like trying to hang out the wash without a clothesline. Write your theme in a single sentence, and tape it above your computer as a reminder of what you're trying to say.

Plot is the story line or action of your romance. Your hero and heroine encounter a series of complications, misunderstandings, or seemingly overwhelming problems that keep them apart.

Eventually, in spite of life's trials, onslaughts, and absurdities, they come to realize what's most important—their relationship with God and each other. Your plot must evolve out of the needs and motivations of your main characters and present a story problem that is crucial to their well being. Remember, conflict is essential to plot.

Your character (usually the heroine in a romance) is the person central to your plot through whom your theme is revealed. Both she and the hero must evoke the reader's empathy and emotion. While the focus is on their relationship, you will still want to show them growing and changing individually through the course of your story.

2. Write a Synopsis of Your Story

In a synopsis, or summary, the main principle is tell, don't show, while in the novel, the rule is, show, don't tell. You don't need a finished plot in mind to begin writing your synopsis. Putting down what you know so far will take you to the point where new material flows into your mind. Using a right-brain, free-writing approach, I write my novel synopses in narrative style, third person, present tense, often adding bits of dialogue, description, or notes for future research as they occur to me.

Later, I edit a polished, shortened version of the synopsis for my publisher; but my original, unedited copy becomes my or road map to guide me in my writing. Remember, while the synopsis summarizes or *tells*, the novel *shows*, immediately drawing the reader into an actual scene filled with sensory details and description.

As you write your synopsis, you might wonder at what point you can be sure you have a well-developed plot. You have a solid, cohesive plot when you can answer these eleven questions:

1. Who is the main character in your story?
2. What is she like as a person—strengths and weaknesses?
3. Who is the hero, plus other key people, who will affect her life?
4. What is the major conflict between the hero and heroine?
5. How do they attempt to resolve the conflict?
6. What obstacles do they encounter in their efforts to resolve their relationship?

7. How do they overcome each obstacle or complication?
8. What is the climax/dramatic turning point of your story?
9. What is the final resolution of your story?
10. What changes occur in your hero and heroine to make their relationship work at last?
11. Why is your story worth telling? (Have a worthy theme.)

Most of my synopses run about ten to twenty pages, double spaced, although the one I submit to a publisher is usually a highly edited, abbreviated version, about four or five pages. Remember, a well-done synopsis will guide and reassure you through the long, lonely labor of birthing a book.

3. Write Character Sketches for All Primary and Secondary Characters

How do I create fictional characters? I begin with feelings and impressions—hazy, shadowy figures in my imagination, without substance or form. I let them germinate in my mind until they take on identities and motivations. When they are ready to be named, I make lists of first and last names from phone books, baby books, or school yearbooks. When I find the right name for a specific character, I go through my extensive picture file looking for his or her face a photo that matches my mental image of my character. Then, armed with name and photo, I go to my computer and, using a free-style, right-brain technique, write an extensive character sketch (two or three pages), probing my character's feelings, needs, motivations, and background.

I include the following information in these case histories:

1. A character's physical appearance: Not just whether he's tall, dark, and handsome or short, fat, and ugly. Rather, what separates him from the masses and makes him unique, one in a million?

2. His personality and temperament: Is he cool and laid back, hot and fiery, aggressive, passive, impulsive, cautious, etc.?

3. His motivations: What makes him act the way he does? What are his felt, or perceived, needs? What are his real needs? What does he desire more than anything else in the world?

4. His background and family history: History tends to repeat itself in generation after generation, as evidenced in the biblical concept of "the sins of the fathers." Beliefs and actions are deeply rooted in the past.

5. His general attitude toward others and himself: Does he accept himself and others? Does he have identity and self-esteem problems to work through?

6. His outlook on life: Is it positive? Negative? Fearful? Reckless? Practical? Romantic?

7. His habits, both good and bad: Habits define him as a character. Does he eat a leisurely breakfast of bacon and eggs or grab a cup of black coffee on the run? Is his desk cluttered or spotless? Does he keep appointments on time or always arrive ten minutes late?

8. His education, profession, and station in life: What does a character's career tell about him, his abilities, interests, and long-range goals? A diplomat or university professor will have different concerns and ways of expressing them than a taxi driver or steelworker. But be wary of stereotypes. Perhaps that diplomat got his start as a taxi driver. And keep in mind that both heroes and heroines in romance novels rarely have boring, mundane jobs.

9. His strengths and weaknesses: Every human personality has both a light and dark side. A balanced mixture of lights and darks creates a three-dimensional character. But keep in mind that some traits can be both strengths and weaknesses. An example is the strong, silent type who refuses to open up and communicate with his mate. Remember, heroes in romances may be flawed, but not deeply. Readers want to love them in spite of their faults.

10. His idiosyncrasies: What gestures or mannerisms are peculiar to this character? Does he pull on his ear, clear his throat, tap his fingers, fidget with his collar, lick his lips, fiddle with his glasses, twist his ring, or shrug his shoulders? (Of course, if he does all these at once, he has a real problem! And, of course, he doesn't belong in a romance novel.)

11. His voice: Avoid the trap of letting all your characters sound alike—like you, the author. Readers "hear" a character's voice in their heads, and they'll cringe if he doesn't sound authentic. Determine what rhythm of speech your character has—smooth, flowing sentences or short and choppy? What tone of voice—soft and mellow, deep, nasal, singsong, melodic, breathy, gravelly, or monotone? Does he have an accent? Use big words to impress people? Speak too loud? Too fast? Or does he speak with a warmth that puts others at ease? Whatever the case, make him a one and only original.

By the time I've explored the personalities of all my characters, I have a clear mental picture of how they relate to and impact one another. It's as if I've put a puzzle together and all the pieces fit.

When I want to explore a character's feelings in depth, I mentally step into his skin and write spontaneously in first person for ten to fifteen minutes without stopping. This instinctive, freewheeling exercise allows you to "discover" your characters' traits by tapping into your own subconscious. Try it. You'll be surprised by what your characters tell you! Such revelations are part of the joy and wonder of writing novels.

4. Break Your Synopsis into Chapters

Be sure something significant happens in each chapter to forward the action. Always include conflict and emotion, with a number of intensely dramatic moments building like stair steps toward the highest point or climax of your story, the point at which everything will be won or lost for your characters.

5. Write Descriptions of Your Novel's Main Locations

Include foreign locales, real or imaginary cities, your own hometown, or even your own living room. Do your homework. Be accurate and vivid in setting the scene, drawing from all five senses to capture your characters in their natural environment. Small but insightful details will hit home with readers, providing they ring of truth that makes your story live and breathe.

Don't trust your memory for such details. Whenever possible, go to the location of your story and videotape or take photographs. If feasible, write out descriptions on the spot.

When Doris Elaine Fell and I coauthored the *Mist Over Morro Bay* series of mystery-romance novels, we selected a cruise ship to Alaska as the setting for our fourth novel, *Beyond the Windswept Sea.* We took Alaskan cruises for our research. I interviewed officers and staff, toured the ship, took pictures, and videotaped a man-over-board drill in the icy waters of Glacier Bay. Did our research pay off? I think so. After reading our book, a woman back from an Alaskan cruise told me, "I enjoyed *your* cruise more than mine!"

If you can't visit the locations in your novel, visit your public library and read about them, or rent videos. Don't just wing it from your armchair, trusting vague generalizations to convey a strong sense of place.

6. *Do Necessary Research on Subjects to Be Covered*

Objective facts must be accurate to sustain the illusion of reality and to give credibility to your emotional details. Research is as vital for fiction (even romances) as for nonfiction.

Since I'm not a fashion expert or a gourmet cook, I select my characters' wardrobes from clothing catalogs and feed them delectable meals from my collection of restaurant menus. I keep a Sears catalog handy to check out shoes, appliances, furniture, and other household items my characters may need. If you want information about something—whether it's a vehicle, an organization, or a disease—there's probably a brochure or catalog somewhere that tells about it.

Naturally, primary sources are better than secondary sources. So don't be satisfied to read a book or article if you can go directly to the source for information. Talk with people who have experience. Interview police officers, lawyers, detectives, psychologists, doctors, nurses, military personnel—anyone who is willing to share his perspective and shed light on topics in your novel.

7. *Begin the Actual Writing*

At any point in these first six steps, you may find yourself compelled to begin writing. Fine. When you're ready, you'll sense it. When that elusive muse nudges or inspires you, seize the opportunity to write. But don't get so caught up in the writing that you neglect your organization and research. Let your story ripen; don't pluck it when it's green. By the same token, don't let your story become overripe. Don't get so caught up in the preparations that you never get around to writing.

If possible, write an entire chapter at a sitting, reviewing your synopsis, character sketches, and research materials as necessary.

Write freely, with minimal editing, visualizing your scenes and letting yourself experience your characters' emotions. Have fun with your story. See your writing as a great adventure that heightens all your senses and makes you prickle with excitement. What you experience as you write is what your reader will experience as she reads. If you feel yourself slogging through the material and barely keeping your head above water, your reader will feel that same sense of drudgery. But if you take pleasure in the writing, your reader will take pleasure in the reading.

8. *Don't Be Afraid to Change Your Outline or Synopsis*

The process of writing is a journey, an adventure, an exploration of the unknown. Your romance novel may take new directions, the characters may evolve differently from what you expected, and the plot may need to be adjusted to accommodate new ideas and revised goals. That's natural.

Don't be anxious. Keep your outline as a loose structure to guide you, but be flexible enough to respond to your own creative instincts and impulses. Your synopsis is a road map to guide you in your travels. Once you begin your journey, you may discover other side roads and avenues more exciting than the path you marked out.

9. *Write the Entire Rough Draft. Then Go Back and Evaluate It and Rewrite as Needed*

An artist would be foolish to finish one small corner of his painting while leaving the rest of the canvas blank. By the same token, don't insist on editing your first few chapters to perfection before tackling the rest of your novel.

Complete the entire rough draft before going back for intensive editing. Why? You may find that your perspective has changed drastically, or your original vision for the work has undergone a transformation. When the entire "picture" is finished, step back and scrutinize the whole.

While you wrote your rough draft in a spontaneous, freewheeling, right-brain mode, you will want to put your "inner critic" in the driver's seat for your rewrite. That's the key word. Be willing to rewrite, rewrite, rewrite! Check spelling, punctuation, grammar, clarity of expression, facts, logic, pacing, style, and tone.

When you've given it all you've got, give your manuscript to someone else to evaluate—another writer, an editor, a critique group, someone whose judgment you trust. Even the most professional writer has tunnel vision and needs the objectivity of another person. Be responsive to criticism, not defensive. Few published writers have thin skin; years of deflecting rejection slips have given most tough hides.

10. Submit a Cover Letter, Three Sample Chapters, and Your Synopsis to a Publisher

Begin submitting your proposal as soon as you have several chapters completed. Try one publisher or several, as long as you let the editors know you are querying several publishers at once. If your proposal interests them, most editors will want to see an entire manuscript from an unpublished novelist. A novelist with several books to her credit may receive a contract on the basis of a proposal.

Your proposal should be as polished and error free as you can make it. First impressions count. In our computer age, there is no excuse for a sloppy manuscript. Enclose a brief letter of introduction (no more than two pages, single-spaced), stating your writing background and qualifications, what your novel is about, and your target audience.

Most publishers want to know six things about your manuscript: subject, purpose, theme, method, importance, and market. When mailing your proposal, put your cover letter first, followed by your synopsis (double-spaced), then your sample chapters (usually the first three, also double-spaced). Don't forget to enclose a stamped, self-addressed return envelope, and pray that the editor won't need it.

Who knows? Your inspirational romance may be the Great American Novel the whole world is waiting to read. Or better yet, it may touch and change someone's heart for all eternity.

Endnotes

1. Carole Gift Page, *Rachel's Hope* (New York: Love Inspired, 1998), p. 100.
2. Carole Gift Page, *In Search of Her Own* (New York: Love Inspired, 1997), p. 251.

CAROLE GIFT PAGE is the author of 40 books and 800 stories and articles. She has published with a dozen major publishers, including Thomas Nelson, Bethany House, Moody, Harvest House, Crossway, Tyndale, Victor Books, Regal, and Steeple Hill. Her romance novels include the Heartland Memories Series (*House on Honeysuckle Lane*, *Home to Willowbrook*, *Hope of Herrick House*, *Storms Over Willowbrook*, Thomas Nelson); *Kara and Carrie* (Bethany House); and four contemporary romances from Steeple Hill: *In Search of Her Own*, *Decidedly Married*, *Rachel's Hope*, and *Stranger in My Home*.

—— 22 ——

Top Ten Rules for Mystery Writers

JAMES SCOTT BELL

I write for the same reason
I breathe—because if I didn't, I would die.
—ISAAC ASIMOV

ALL GOOD STORIES ARE MYSTERIES. An author wants readers wondering what is going to happen next, delaying final answers so the reader will continue to turn pages. That's what makes books sell. This fact is especially true for mystery stories. Like any genre, it has conventions. These can be modified or ignored, of course, but first they must be understood. And it all starts with...

RULE #1: YOU HAVE TO HAVE A SECRET

With no secret there is no mystery. Simple enough, isn't it? There has to be a deep, dark secret that permeates the entire book. And since you want readers to care enough to read the whole story, you have to make the secret a doozy.

In the murder mystery, the secret is always: Who did it? Someone has been murdered, and the detective or lead character has to find the murderer. Or there may be some other violent act—a bombing, for instance—which triggers the story, and the question is: Who planted the bomb?

But at the very least, the secret must be compelling. Why? Because in a mystery, there has to be a compelling reason for the hero to solve a case. Trying to find grandma's missing pajamas is not exactly riveting. Finding her murderer is. This problem, by the way, is the main rule that distinguishes mysteries from thrillers. Thrillers usually involve the threat of violence or death. In a mystery, the main character needs something to solve. While the two genres can borrow from each other (I always try to put a little mystery in my thrillers), they can be separated this way.

It's not enough, however, just to plant a secret.

Rule #2: The Secret Has to Be Planted Early

Good mysteries and suspense stories start quickly. Sometimes the author chooses to make the first chapter the crime and the rest of the book the solution. I chose this path in my legal thriller *Circumstantial Evidence*. The book begins with a murder. The next chapter switches to a scene with my heroine in a totally unrelated context. When the two story lines merge, the rest of the book takes off. Sometimes the author starts with the hero in action. This was my choice in *Final Witness*. The advantage is that readers know who to root for right away. Just make sure the next chapter involves the incident that gets the plot rolling.

Whatever action you choose for the inciting incident, give it to the reader as soon as you can. There is a good rule that applies to any kind of fiction: Don't warm up your engines. Especially in a mystery.

Once you have the action rolling, it follows naturally that...

Rule #3: Somebody Has to Solve the Mystery

This fact seems self-evident, but note that little phrase "has to." For a mystery to reach out and grab readers, the hero has to have a stake in solving the problem. The higher the stakes, the greater the reader interest.

In a detective story, the stake is the professional reputation of the investigator. He must solve the mystery because, quite simply, that is what he does for a living. When people came to Sherlock Holmes, it was because of his reputation as the greatest sleuth in the world. And Holmes made solving his cases a point of personal pride. With a series character, this is almost always the reason they want to solve cases. That's their job.

You can add a level of compulsion (and marketability) by giving your hero a personal stake. If it is the hero's father who is murdered, the stakes rise. If the whole family starts dropping off, and it looks like the hero could be next, you have to have a page-turning premise.

But the mystery cannot be solved right away because…

RULE #4: THINGS HAVE TO GET WORSE FOR THE HERO

A venerable rule of good fiction is this: Get your hero up a tree. Throw rocks at him. Then get him down. Trouble for the hero is the engine of readable fiction. Readers like to worry about their heroes. So don't let your hero have an easy time solving the mystery. (There is a sub-rule here that is often missed by beginning writers, but is absolutely crucial to a good mystery: The villain must be just as clever as the hero.)

In fact, just about every step the hero takes should put him in a worse position. The threats mount, the case seems more confusing, key witnesses disappear. Only when it all looks hopeless, as if there is no way the mystery will ever be resolved, does the solution present itself. But that solution will only be satisfying if you observe…

RULE #5: YOU MUST DEAL FAIRLY WITH THE READERS

Never, ever, cheat your readers with a solution they could never anticipate. There are no coincidental endings in good mystery writing. (In fact, a good rule to remember is that any coincidence you use in a story should be used against the hero).

The mark of a good mystery is a solution that seems inevitable, yet was not anticipated. This technique is hard to do, and that's why writers shouldn't dash off mysteries in an afternoon. Your opening chapter may sell your book, but your ending is what sells your next book.

So how do you make a surprising ending seem inevitable? You follow…

RULE #6: YOU MUST PLANT CLUES

While many mystery writers outline extensively before they start to write, there are others who don't know "who did it" when they start typing. And there are those who plan to have a certain character as the killer, only to end up with it being somebody else entirely. So the confused writer might ask, "How do I know what clues to plant if I don't know who does it?" The answer is simple: plant the clues *after* you finish writing.

Yes, this procedure is permissible. It's your story. It is easy to do and also allows you, because you now see the big picture, to keep those clues from being too obvious.

There is another way to go about this clue business, and that's to let your imagination run free during the first draft. What you may find, as I have, is that your mind starts suggesting that odd little things be dropped in, even though you don't know why. Sometimes those odd things don't go anywhere, but other times they are a result of your creative mind running ahead of you, saying "I've got this neat clue and payoff in mind, so just trust me, will you? Put this in the story now, and you'll see how it comes into play later. Won't you just do me that little favor, pal? Goodness knows, I've done enough favors for you." Listen to the suggestions your creative mind makes. That's its job.

It has another job as well, and that is to help you…

Rule #7: Create Great Leading Characters

Every mystery plot has been written, of course. That is, the essential plot paradigms have all been used before. So what is the secret of a fresh, engaging mystery? Great characters! Without interesting, wonderful, three-dimensional characters, you will have a tired mystery with cardboard cutouts walking through too-familiar territory.

Your first task as a mystery writer is to establish a reader bond with your lead character. You must give readers a reason to keep turning pages, and the best reason is always that they are emotionally invested in the lead character. Writing teacher Jack Bickham says readers want to *worry* about what happens to the main character. Worry comes only when readers find something in the lead to care about. To accomplish that, your lead must be two things: interesting and sympathetic.

How do you come up with an interesting lead? Many writers like to do lengthy character biographies. Personally, I like to see and hear my lead as soon as possible. I try to form a mental image and then fill in the following information: name, occupation, dominant impression one would get when meeting this person, a philosophy of life, and one major turning point from childhood. Then I force myself to answer this question: Why do I love this character? Until I can come up with a convincing answer, I'm not ready to write about my lead.

Next, give your lead one of the five dominant drives: adventure, security, recognition, response, power. One of these drives will motivate the lead and give him a general direction throughout the story.

As for sympathy, you can establish that in a number of ways. Here are the best:

1. *Jeopardy:* The reader tends to root for anyone facing immediate danger.

2. *Hardship:* Terrible circumstances—environmental, physical, mental, spiritual—always bring out the sympathy factor.

3. *Vulnerability:* Look for those areas of your lead's inner character or outer situation, where he might be affected in harmful ways.

4. *Likability:* This simply means having your lead do likable things. In screenwriting, one often hears about the "pet the dog" beat. That's where a tough guy, when no on is looking, bends down and pets a scraggly dog. That little action shows us an attractive side of the lead we might not have seen otherwise.

Work hard on making your leads deep and interesting—but not perfect! Allow them some freedom to move in your imagination. For me, writing gets most exciting when my characters start to take over, and I just follow them around.

Your job isn't finished with a great lead, however; you also need to…

RULE #8: CREATE COLORFUL MINOR CHARACTERS

The hero of your story will need some help to attain his goal. He will need people who act as close friends and confidants or experts in some area. There may be a love interest for the hero as well, someone to motivate him to action. These are all minor characters. If you want your story to shine, you need to color them interesting. Some minor characters play a more important role than others, so spend a great deal of time with them. Give them strong passions, traits, opinions, and habits. Don't allow them to be drab. Then there are characters who are required just to move the story along. But there is no need for them to be bland. In fact, you can spice up your story by making sure each minor character is individualized.

How do you do that? By giving each character tags. A tag is something the character does or says, something other characters (and the reader, of course) can see. It distinguishes the character, makes him different from the others. Tags include patterns of speech, dress, physical appearance, mannerisms, tics, eccentricities, and so forth. These set characters apart. And because there are an almost infinite variety of tags, you can make every single one of your characters a unique individual. Just like life.

Tags will also help you avoid the biggest mistake writers make with characters—writing them as clichés. You know what I mean: the stocky, macho truck driver; the tough-talking waitress; the cigar-chewing New York cabby; the shy, mousy accountant.

Don't take the easy route. You can change a tag here and there, even going to the opposite extreme, and come up with a fresh character every time.

Each time you have to come up with a minor character, ask: What is his purpose in the story? What tags can I attach to him? How can I make each tag unique or memorable?

Once you have great characters, you're ready to…

Rule #9: Tie Up All the Loose Ends

In a good mystery, there is a sense that everything important has been explained, that there are no threads still hanging. Nothing is worse for a reader than turning pages breathlessly, only to find the ending disappointing.

It's a good idea to keep a list in front of you with all the major story points. These come up in your planning and in the actual writing, and you need to know what they are at all times. I keep these notes in my actual text, at the bottom of my computerized document. For example, I'll write a note like this: Maybe Bosley has important information he refuses to give, and that's why Selma is confused. This tells me that at some point I have to deal with this item, and I won't forget about it.

And just to make sure I leave the readers happy, I always…

RULE #10: REWRITE RUTHLESSLY

It's true that great writing is rewriting. The best mystery writers don't get everything right in one draft, so chances are you won't either.

After a first draft, set the manuscript aside for a week or so; then read through it with a fresh mind. Jot only occasional notes. Your question is: How does the story read as a whole?

Then go through the story again with a checklist of questions. Here are a few I use:

- Is the mystery important enough? Will readers care?
- Is my hero sympathetic? If not, revise the character.
- Does my hero show moral courage?
- Can my hero quit the story at any time? If so, make it so he can't.
- What characters can be combined or eliminated?
- Do characters sufficiently contrast?
- Are the minor characters colorful?
- Do they relate to the plot?
- Do I start the novel off with a bang?
- Is there conflict in almost every scene?
- Do subplots connect?
- Do I need a minor subplot in the middle to increase pressure and interest?
- Can I set a "ticking clock" for the last third of the story?
- Do all the characters have a purpose (goal) in each scene?
- Do my scenes have urgency? Time pressure?
- Is the opposition strong enough?

Now write a second draft. Give this draft to a few trusted friends, ones who won't be shy about giving you their opinions. Don't be afraid of criticism—it's the only way to learn. Take what they say and see if you agree. Then fix the problems. That's what the process of rewriting is all about.

This chapter alone won't enable you to write a great mystery, but it will help. If you take this advice and couple it with an intense desire to write a good story—and if you keep on learning about the craft and keep on writing, writing, writing— soon you'll have readers staying up into the night, turning pages, dying to know what happens next.

Then your success won't be a mystery. It will be earned.

JAMES SCOTT BELL has written over 300 articles and numerous books for the legal profession. A former trial lawyer, he is the author of the legal thrillers *Circumstantial Evidence* and *Final Witness*, both from Broadman & Holman, and is currently under contract for three more novels. Jim has taught screenwriting at The Master's College, novel writing at Learning Tree University in Los Angeles, and the art and craft of fiction at various writers conferences. He writes a regular column called "Top Performance" for the *Daily Journal*, California's leading legal newspaper and publishes the monthly newsletter *Trial Excellence*. He lives in the San Fernando Valley (CA) with his wife, son, and daughter.

— 23 —

Historical Fiction: Creating a Narrative Tapestry

JACK CAVANAUGH

History will be kind to me
for I intend to write it.
—WINSTON CHURCHILL

THE *APOCALYPSE* IS BY FAR ONE of the grandest examples of tapestry art ever created. Begun in 1377 by Nicolas Bataille, it is a set of seven, enormous, handwoven panels, each measuring approximately 16 feet high and 80 feet long. The subject of this massive effort is the biblical revelation received by the Apostle John on the Isle of Patmos. Bataille used a total of 105 separate scenes to depict this wonderfully visual prophecy.

What Bataille has done with needle and thread, the writer of historical fiction does with words. We recreate dramatic scenes from a previous era. And, like makers of tapestries, we have a variety of colorful strands from which to choose. Two are primary to our task: historical fact and imaginative fiction. The amount of each strand and its placement in the overall narrative is the creative task of the author.

THE HISTORICAL STRAND

A writer of historical fiction would do well to keep one important fact in mind: People hate history. They always have. French philosopher Pascal called history a perpetual conspiracy against the truth. Napoleon asked, "What is history but a fable agreed upon?" And Sir Robert Walpole was even more direct when he stated flatly, "History must be false."

While it is readily acknowledged that people in general don't like history, surely this point doesn't apply to readers of historical fiction, does it? Don't be too sure. Think about it. When was the last time you saw a history book on a best-seller list? Or when was the last time you saw someone at the beach, on an airplane, or in a restaurant reading a history text for pleasure? Make no mistake about it. Readers of historical fiction, like everyone else, hate history.

Yet it is not uncommon to find historical novels on best-seller lists or to see people reading them in droves in public places. Why? The answer is simple. The authors of these books don't write history. They write about people who lived in another time and place. The difference is worth noting.

A number of years ago, *Time* took a survey of their readership. The editors wanted to know which parts of their publication were read most often. To their surprise, one section stood out above all the others. It was the single page of celebrity anecdotes. As a result of the survey, they launched *People*, one of the most popular magazines on the market today. The editors stumbled on a significant truth. People enjoy reading stories about other people. Anyone who desires to write historical fiction would do well to learn this lesson too.

While a well-meaning novice might begin his American Revolutionary War novel with a detailed accounting of the grievous acts of Parliament that culminated in 342 chests of tea being dumped unceremoniously into Boston Harbor, a successful novelist would choose a more personal approach. He might depict a young, unshaved Benedict Arnold moping around a Caribbean tavern, lovesick to the point of incapacity, perilously delaying the return voyage of his merchant ships week after week in the vain hope that an arriving ship might bear a letter from his wife—a letter she never writes.

This is a story people will read. Why? Because the tale of a lovesick man is more interesting than an accounting of historical facts. Readers want to get caught up in people's lives. An author can receive no greater compliment than that which is given to

Margaret Mitchell every time a devoted fan walks into the Atlanta Visitor Center and asks for directions to the grave sites of Scarlett O'Hara and Rhett Butler.

History As Character

With this point in mind, weave the historical strand of your narrative tapestry with great care. Here is the key: Treat history as a character. Have your fictional characters interact with the historical events, persons, and culture of their day. Let this interaction define who they are. Let it challenge them and change them.

It is this interaction that sets historical fiction apart from period fiction. Writers of period fiction use history as a setting. For them, the past is nothing more than a backdrop, a dash of flavoring or a splash of color. Their story could be told just as easily in Arthurian England as it could be on the ancient steppes of Kazakhstan. Contrarily, for true historical fiction, separating a character from his place and time would be like severing Siamese twins.

So now the question is, "How much history is enough, and how much is too much?" Quite frankly, the answer to this question is a matter of taste. My novels have more history in them than other novels on the market. I have chosen a greater emphasis on history intentionally, fully aware of the risk I'm taking, considering that people don't like history. At times I've pulled it off successfully. At times I haven't.

When I first began writing novels, I asked five different readers to critique my manuscripts. I chose my readers carefully. One loves historical fiction; she was able to compare my writing to other historical fiction authors. One loves romances; she let me know what to expect from my female readers. One was a technical writer and a close friend; he gave me a male point of view. And two were housewives who openly acknowledged their dislike for history; they were my litmus test. If they wrote, "too much history" or "boring" in the margins, I knew the history professor inside me was butting into the story. On the other hand, when comments such as, "this is good" or "I didn't know that" appeared in what I considered a history section, I knew that I was on target. My readers were confirming that I had woven historical matter into the flow of the story without interrupting it. This is the goal of the author when using the historical strand.

Details

The essence of the historical strand is detail. A detail is said to be concrete if it appeals to the five senses. In preparation for writing a scene, I like to step into the scene myself and slowly turn around. I ask myself: What do I see? Smell? Taste? Hear? What textures can I run my fingers across? Do this in brainstorming fashion by writing down everything that comes to mind regardless of whether or not you think you'll use it. Take your time. Don't end this exercise prematurely. Lingering often yields the richest sensory discoveries.

Once the brainstorming is complete, the next task at hand is to select the appropriate details for the scene. There was a time when writers could spend five to seven pages describing a room. Those days are long gone. What details should you choose for your scene? Choose only significant ones.

Significant details convey an idea or judgment or both. Ask yourself, "What emotion am I attempting to evoke in this scene? Do I want the reader to laugh? Do I want her to cry? Or do I want her to sense that something is not right?" Then choose only the details that will help strike such a mood. For example, what mood would the following details suggest: the hollow ticking of a clock; an unseen cat's childlike moan; chill bumps rising on one's skin; the musty scent of an old attic; shadows that stretch across the room, covering boxes and old furniture like a shroud? These are details that establish an eerie, foreboding mood, a scene of apprehension in which the reader fears what might be lurking down a hallway or behind a locked closet door. Don't be satisfied with just any detail. Use significant details to create a mood.

The Fiction Strand

When I first started writing fiction, I attended a host of writers' conferences. My goal was not to learn fiction techniques. I figured I could learn technique by reading and studying novels. I went hoping to meet the people who would be making decisions about whether or not to publish my fiction. I figured if I knew what they were looking for, I could tailor my narrative tapestry accordingly.

At the end of one long conference day, several of us dragged ourselves to a final late night session in a campus lounge for an informal question-and-answer period with a respected fiction editor. Knowing that such an opportunity comes along infrequently, I had made a list of questions to ask. At the top of my list was this one: "What is the first thing you look for when you pick up an author's manuscript?"

Without hesitation, he replied, "I want the author to draw me into his world."

Good advice. A writer of historical fiction should not assume his readers are familiar with the story's setting, be it Civil War America or prehistoric France. It is the author's first and greatest task not only to introduce the reader to that world but to lure her into it, to transport her back in time to a world that is as alien to her as twentieth century America would be to Julius Caesar.

Levels of Involvement

There is one particular fiction technique that has the ability to accomplish such a task. It is based on the observation that there are four levels of involvement. Say, for example, you picked up the newspaper and read that there was a car crash on a major interstate freeway near your home. Unless it was a fifty-car pileup, you probably wouldn't take much notice. Cars crash on freeways every day. This is the fourth level of involvement. It is furthest from the action. The only tie you have to the crash is that it involves human beings who travel in cars, and you are a human being who sometimes travels in a car.

Now let's say that you come home from work, and your neighbor meets you in your driveway. His face is ashen. He tells you about this horrible crash he witnessed on the freeway. He describes the scene. A car tumbled over and over right in front of him. The people inside were tossed around like clothes in a dryer. There was the smell of gasoline. The car was on fire. As he recounts the screams of the victims inside the car, his voice quivers. Tears come to his eyes. He's obviously shaken by the accident. This is the third level of involvement. You're closer to the action this time. You know an eyewitness to the accident.

Taking the analogy one step further, now suppose that you are the eyewitness. You saw the car tumbling. You smelled the gasoline.

You saw the fire. You were the one pulling on jammed doors trying to free the victims inside. You heard their screams. This is the second level of involvement. You are closer to the action than before, but as a bystander you are still one step removed.

Now imagine you are in the car that is tumbling. Sky and ground are reversed, righted, and reversed again. You feel the fire that is only inches away from your flesh. You smell gasoline. It is your children's screams that are coming from the back seat. Your legs kick frantically at jammed doors to free them. You see the distorted faces of rescuers through the mosaic of shattered glass. You've heard about freeway fatalities; now you wonder if you're about to become one. This is the first level of involvement, the level that is closest to the action. It is at this level where everything is felt most keenly. Senses are heightened; emotions intense.

How do you draw readers into your world? Put them in the car.

Point of View

Ask yourself, "In whose head is the camera?" This becomes your point of view person for that scene. Then write everything through the eyes and senses of that person. Everything said and done in that scene should be strained through the mesh of that person's experience and bias. In this way readers experience the scene, they don't just read about it. They enter the book on a level of involvement that is closest to the action.

Prewriting

Another thing to remember when using your fiction strand is to plan out the tapestry before you start weaving. Granted, there are some writers who begin with little or no preparation. Maybe I'm missing their particular genius, but I can't imagine a weaver of tapestry beginning his creation without a cartoon (preparatory design), and I can't fathom writing a novel without significant prewriting.

Before writing the first word of a novel, your major characters have to be well drawn. Doing so is a time-consuming process and, at times, a frustrating one. But if you don't know your characters intimately, how can you portray them with any semblance to flesh and blood?

To assist me in this process, I've collected a list of questions that I use to shape each major character. This list includes questions about their physical attributes, family background and upbringing, emotional make-up, spiritual condition, goals, quirks, and fantasies. Yes, these characteristics are a lot of work. Often when working through the questionnaire, I'll cry out something like, "How should I know what her favorite flavor of ice cream is?" But persistent effort inevitably yields an answer, and then I know something about my character I didn't know before.

Plotting is another area that requires extensive prewriting. Begin by choosing the time period in which your story will take place. Then select historical events, places, and people with which your characters will interact. Next explore fictional characters that are at risk in this particular time, and search for story ideas that are fraught with drama and danger. Once your characters are selected ask yourself, "What is the worst possible thing that could happen to him growing out of his greatest fear?" The answer becomes the climax of the book and your writing target.

Once you have a target, you have something at which to aim. From that moment on, everything—including the first sentence—points at that target. If a scene or character doesn't significantly move the action toward the mark, don't use it. Your target will keep you from wandering far afield and stumbling down dead-end streets.

Having completed the prewriting process, you're ready to begin writing. You know your characters, the world in which they'll interact, and the great crisis that looms on the horizon. This point is where you don your storyteller's hat and begin weaving your literary tapestry.

CONCLUSION

I once read a story about a Chinese man who was world renown for his exquisite tapestries. Students flocked to learn from this master craftsman. However, none of the students were able to match their teacher's brilliance. The man's critics accused him of deliberately withholding the best materials and techniques from his students. The master replied, "My students and I use the same silk thread and the same stitches."

His critics challenged him: "Then how do you account for the fact that your tapestries are so superior?"

The master replied, "The difference between my students and me is that I have found the golden needle."

The golden needle in Chinese folklore refers to one's own creativity. Blessed is the writer who discovers his own golden needle and then uses it to the glory of God.

JACK CAVANAUGH is the author of the award-winning historical fiction series An American Family Portrait (Chariot Victor), which concluded in 1999 with book seven, *The Peacemakers*. He has also authored the African Covenant Series (Moody). He is currently working on several other series which are scheduled to appear in 1999. In addition to his writing, Jack is a popular inspirational speaker and an ordained Baptist pastor. He lives with his wife and children in Chula Vista, California.

— 24 —

Selling What You Write

SALLY E. STUART

The free-lance writer is a man who is paid per piece or per word or perhaps.

—ROBERT BENCHLEY

MARKETING IS A WORD THAT OFTEN strikes terror in the hearts of experienced as well as novice writers. Yet it is the part of the process that ultimately defines us as successful or simply wanna-be's. For that reason, the goal of this chapter is to try to take some of the mystique out of the process and lead you, step-by-step, toward that success.

The interesting thing about marketing is that most of us know more about it than we realize. If you have ever worked in a job that involves selling any kind of a product, you can take what you know and put it to work in marketing your manuscripts. A manuscript, after all, is just another product looking for a buyer. So what is it you already know about marketing? What about the principles of supply and demand? How can you know your customer, and how do you reach him—keeping up with his changing needs? Think about everything you have learned about selling successfully.

Let's assume you are going to start a new business selling software, cookies, or bird houses. Before you start, you will find out everything you can about the need for your particular product, how to reach the customer, what the customer is looking for, who your competition is, and all the other concerns that come into play with your particular product. You would never open up shop in a random location without first studying all these factors critical to your success.

As I remind people in my marketing classes, you would not make a dress or any custom-made product and then go door-to-door looking for someone to buy it. The smart business person will find out what the customer wants and create a product to fit.

Yet many writers approach marketing like the person going door-to-door. They write a manuscript and then start shopping it from one editor to another, looking for one who needs something with that particular slant and length, who hasn't already published something like it, who is looking for manuscripts, who can afford to buy something right now, etc. It is no wonder they face rejection after rejection. Once you view writing as a business and approach the marketplace in a businesslike manner, you will sell your manuscripts like Mrs. Fields sells cookies.

A Marketing Plan

Every successful business starts with a marketing plan, and your writing business needs one too. For years I have been teaching a plan that has worked to make countless writers successful. You can use the same principles to create a plan that works for you. It is not difficult, but it does take time and a commitment to follow it through to success. As long as you have a marketable product, the plan will successfully identify and connect you to your customers.

If you are just beginning to write for publication, there will be a natural period of exploration in which you try a number of different topics or types of writing to discover what you can do best, what sells, what you enjoy, etc. You might start with poetry, then try some short stories, devotionals, children's material, or feature articles. During that process you will begin to recognize those areas that seem to work best for you or the ones you feel most comfortable pursuing.

This is a process is one we all go through and one you won't want to rush, so don't feel frustrated if you are not ready yet to take the first step in the plan as presented in the next paragraph. The basic concepts will still work while you are finding your niche.

For those who are past that beginner phase, it is time to make decisions about what product you are going to offer. You certainly don't have to limit it to one area, but it is best if you can focus on two or three specific topics or types of writing. The reason for focusing is so you will ultimately be recognized as an expert on certain topics or types of writing. Since the ultimate goal for most of us is to have editors come to us with assignments, we must begin establishing a reputation as a writer with specific skills. If you write on a wide variety of topics and in diverse areas, your name will never be connected to one or more specialties.

If you plan to write books later, it always helps to develop these areas of expertise in periodicals first. Often that gives you enough credibility to write those books, even when you don't have any formal background or education in the topic area. So, for now, decide where you are going to position yourself during the next three to five years.

Along with determining what topics or types of writing you are going to pursue, it is also important to identify your target audience. Who exactly are you writing for? Many writers make the mistake of not targeting closely enough. You can no longer write just for children or adults, you must select one or more specific segments of any market. Children's markets are always broken down by age groups (i.e., ages two and three, four and five, six to eight, eight to twelve); and if you write for children as a single market, you will have a hard time selling your manuscript. There will be no definable target.

The same point is true of adult markets, which are often broken into stages of life, such as college, young adult, singles, early family, later family, empty nest, senior adults, as well as specialty audiences, such as women, men, or pastors. Based on the topics and types of writing you are pursuing, determine what different audiences you are qualified to write for.

Once you have selected your specific topics or types of writing and your audiences, the next step is to determine where you are going to find your potential customers (the publishers).

As I mentioned before, you want to identify your customers first; then custom design your product to fit their particular needs. To find those customers, look up the topic/type in the topical listings in the annual *Christian Writers' Market Guide*. Those listings will tell you specifically which publishers have said they are looking for that type of material; but don't automatically assume that every publisher listed for that topic will fit what you have to offer. Your job now is to go through a process of selection and elimination to determine which markets will be open to your material.

Steps to Follow

In the market guide, read the primary listing for each publisher on your topical list. As you do, watch for clues that indicate if this is or is not a market for you. Cross off any that are disqualified after this initial reading. Often the descriptive statements or tips at the end of most listings will give an indication that your material won't fit some of the markets.

For those still on the list, find in your files, locate on the Internet, or send for a copy of the publication and their writers' guidelines. Read the copy or copies cover to cover and read the guidelines carefully, highlighting any statements that indicate this is or is not a potential market. Again, decide whether to leave this market on your list or cross it off. What you're doing is refining a list of the most likely publishers for each of your topics or types of writing.

Analyze Each Periodical

Now go back and look more closely at the sample copies of the publications still on your list. Pay particular attention to the material that corresponds to what you will want to sell them, such as a feature article, short story, or poetry. Find as many examples of each type and analyze them for specific traits or content. If it's poetry, then note the topics, average length, type of poetry, etc.

The market guide or the writers' guidelines will likely give some information on what they are looking for, but it helps to see what they actually use. If it's a short story, check out the elements that seem to be present in most of the stories they publish. For a feature or major article, make notes of what features are included, such as number of anecdotes, case studies, statistics, quotes from authorities, personal experiences, and any other elements that give the piece credibility beyond the author's opinion.

If the periodical has advertisements, try to determine who the ads are targeting. If there are letters to the editor, read those to see what you can learn about the readers. Are they conservative, liberal, mostly women, mostly pastors, or professionals, etc.? What topics turn them on—or off?

Check the contents page to see the average number of words used in a title. You will find that the titles vary in length for each publication, but they will tend to find a typical range. For example, articles in a scholarly or specialized magazine may have titles eight to ten words (more descriptive), while pieces in a teen publication will have one- or two-word titles (short and punchy).

As you are doing this market analysis, make your own notes on a separate sheet of paper or on the guidelines if room permits. Always write down any information, or even subtle impressions about the publication, as it comes to you. You are seeking clues that will give you insight into what the editors want and ways you can tailor your submissions to fit their established criteria. Also be on the lookout for any specific knowledge about the publication that you can use in your query or cover letter to indicate to the editor that you have done your homework. For example, "Because your primary reading audience is women ages twenty to forty-five...." Or "Because you prefer a humorous, anecdotal approach...." That kind of informed presentation always gets an editor's attention.

By the time you reach this point, you should have a list of several—and sometimes dozens—of markets carefully selected for your target audience, topics, or types of writing. Your choices now have been made on careful market analysis, not wild guesses; and your results will reflect that almost immediately.

So next time you have a great idea you want to write, go to the list of markets you have developed for that type of material and decide first where you are going to send it. You can then plan the slant, length, and style based on what you know about that publication and its audience.

ANALYZE THE BOOK MARKET

You may be wondering how this process works if your interest is in books and not periodicals. Let me say first that I suggest every writer start with articles—even if your ultimate goal is to move into book writing. Much of what you need to learn about writing and marketing you learn best by writing articles. You polish your writing skills, become familiar with the industry and how it operates, and establish your reputation and credibility as a writer. Once you have done that, you're more likely to be noticed and taken seriously by book publishers who have come to prefer working with established writers.

Now you can start the same kind of market research you have done with the magazines. Select the topics or types of books you want to target. (You may want to do your research one topic at a time as you select a topic for each book.) Find the corresponding topical list in the market guide and go through the same process of elimination. Instead of sample copies, you will want to study catalogs. Just as a sample copy will give you a clearer picture of what each publication wants, the catalog will help you find the publishers who are most likely to be interested in your book idea.

There are several steps involved in studying a catalog. Look first at the overall content to see what kinds of books they publish. Would you be comfortable having your book included in this catalog? Some writers are uncomfortable with a publisher that carries books on other religions or religious points of view; others consider their books to be "salt and light" in such a catalog. You must determine your own comfort level.

If it's a house you're comfortable with, look for the section or for other books that deal with your proposed topic. Let's say you want to write a book on marriage. Does the publisher do a large number of marriage books? If so (and you want one that does), do they have another book on the same aspect of marriage you plan to cover? If so, cross this publisher off your list. You are looking for one that has several books on marriage but not one on the same aspect. Typically, a publisher will not publish a book that is in direct competition to one already in their line.

When you find those publishers who have a slot for your book, go to a Christian bookstore to continue your research. Find the section on that topic and see which publishers have the most books on the shelves. Those should be at the top of your list. Check out the books for those, and any other publishers on your list, and evaluate them from a visual standpoint. Which ones are most appealing, as far as covers, design, type style, etc.? Make notes on both positives and negatives.

This is also a good time to find and make a list of books on the same topic you are considering. Ask the book buyer which titles are most popular or which they recommend. If you don't have access to them elsewhere, buy the top two or three to read. Unless you know what is already available, you won't know whether there is a need for your book or if it has already been written.

While you're in the store and talking with the book buyer, ask some additional questions. Which publishers would you think of in relationship to my topic? How do those publishers rate as far as getting books to the store or the distributor when you need them? Also ask any other questions specific to your project. Book buyers are very knowledgeable and will be happy to share their expertise.

A bookstore is also a good place to go if you have an unusual product and are not sure which publisher might be interested. Maybe you are thinking of a gift book with several gift products to go with it. In a bookstore, you can look for other books with accompanying products and find out who has published them. Just be sure your topic area is different than what they already have.

By now you should have a pretty good idea of which publishers you want to target with your book proposal. But first ask yourself very honestly: Does the world need another book of this type or on this topic? If your answer is not a resounding yes, then move on to another topic and repeat the same steps.

CONCLUSION

Obviously the above steps are going to take a commitment of time and energy; but like any other business, marketing must take a good portion of your time if you are going to be successful. To ignore it, or treat it as an afterthought, will almost guarantee failure. The good news is that once you master these steps, they will become almost second nature. And as you become well acquainted with the publishers you have chosen to target, they will soon seem like old friends. And may those friendships be long and prosperous.

Sally E. Stuart has been a writer for thirty-two years and a full-time freelancer for sixteen. She is the author of twenty-four books, including the fourteenth annual *Christian Writers' Market Guide* (Harold Shaw), and has sold over 900 articles and columns. Her involvement with the market guide, as well as her marketing columns for *The Christian Communicator*, *Oregon Christian WRITERS*, and *Advanced Christian Writer*, makes her the leading authority on Christian markets and the business of writing. She is a popular speaker at writers' conferences nationwide. Sally is married, the mother of two sons and a daughter, and the grandmother of eight. You may contact her at 1647 SW Pheasant Drive, Aloha, OR 97006; phone: 503-642-9844; fax: 503-848-3658; e-mail: stuartcwmg@aol.com; Web site: www.stuartmarket.com.

— 25 —

Speaking and Writing: Like a Hand in a Glove

MARITA LITTAUER

Next to the originator of a sentence is the first quoter of it.
—RALPH WALDO EMERSON

KNOWN MORE FOR MY EXPERTISE in speaking than in writing, I was a bit nervous about being invited to speak at my first writers' conference. Wanting to do a good job, I researched my topic well. The week before the conference, I attended the annual Christian Booksellers Association (CBA) Convention. I spoke to many publishers' representatives from companies both large and small, and they all gave me the same advice.

That first evening at the writers' conference, I was asked to say a few words about the sessions I would be teaching: Promoting Yourself as a Speaker and Author, From a Speech to a Book, and Speaking to Promote Your Book. I have expertise in all three areas.

Since this was a writers' conference, many of the people there wondered why they had invited me to teach on speaking. (In looking over the topics in this book, you may have wondered the same thing.) When I shared what I had learned from the publishers, a hush fell over the room. What they said may come as a surprise to you too.

I told the audience, "I have just come from the CBA convention where I spoke to many publishers. They all agreed they would rather publish a less-gifted writer who is marketable than literary art by someone who never intends to leave her computer. What this means is that if you are out there speaking, creating a demand for your message, publishers will be interested in you."

If you have the opportunity to meet with a publisher at a writers' conference, at CBA, or an event like the CLASS (Christian Leaders, Authors & Speakers Services) Reunion, or if you send an editor a manuscript in which he is interested, one of the first questions he will ask you is, "How often are you speaking?" or "How many books will you buy to sell at your events?"

While good writing is important, do not neglect the value of being marketable, of being a speaker, in your quest to get published as the two go together like a hand in a glove. I actually advise people to speak first and then write.

Test Your Material

When you speak first, you have the opportunity to test your material and see if there is public interest. I remember having some new material I thought was great. I envisioned giving seminars all over the country and writing a book on the same topic. I did TV and radio interviews on the subject. I called groups and offered my seminar free so I could try out the material.

I gave the seminar several times free. After that, however, no one ever called and invited me to give that series of presentations again. I had this program listed on my promotional material; and I continued to receive speaking invitations, but not on that topic. How grateful I am that I had not taken the time to write my messages in a book, find a publisher, get it published, and then find out that no one was really interested in the subject.

Additionally, when you speak first, you can refine your material and gather stories from other people who relate to your message and share with you. Each time you present a new topic, be sure to use evaluation forms or comment cards to gather input from audience members. Ask them what parts of the program were the most helpful or meaningful. Ask if there was an area on which they would have liked more time spent. As you give the presentation again and again, you can continually adjust your speech to meet the needs of your audience.

Once you have it refined, have too much material for the given time frame, are continually getting great feedback, and have people asking if you have a book on that topic, you know you are ready to write the book. If you have already polished and refined your material by speaking first, sitting down to write the book is merely a matter of gluing yourself to the keyboard and pretending that you have an audience who wants to hear everything you have to say on the subject, wants to hear every story, and wants complete instructions.

SPEAK FIRST, THEN PUBLISH

Many people have the misconception that no one will want them to speak unless they are published. This couldn't be further from the truth. At CLASS we represent nearly 150 different Christian speakers. I estimate only a third of those speakers are published. Yet many are popular speakers.

One of our most popular speakers has been booked by CLASS for years but has only recently been published. However, once her book came out, her invitations for speaking have come from all over the country, whereas previously the majority of her speaking was in her local area. Being published is an important part of the mix as being an author gives you national recognition as a speaker and increases your demand. So speaking and writing really do go together.

If you are already comfortable speaking and are interested in getting published, start now. Getting a book published, however, is a lengthy process, usually involving several years.

LEARN TO SPEAK

If you feel you lack the skills needed to speak, you can learn them at the CLASSeminar (held five times a year throughout the country and available on tape) or by joining Toastmasters International. You can also read *Talking So People Will Listen* and my chapter in *The Complete Guide to Christian Writing and Speaking*.

If you already have a book published, you, too, need to be speaking. Speaking sells books! That's why publishers ask about your speaking and factor that into their decision of whether or not to publish your work.

Create an Information Sheet

To get started in speaking—assuming you already know how to speak and you have a message that people want to hear—begin by creating an information sheet. This sheet is a one-page flyer (front and back if needed) that contains your biographical information, your listing of available topics with a short description of each message, quotes about your speaking (if you have them), and information on how to contact you. Assuming you are speaking to a Christian audience, the biographical information should be more of your testimony than a listing of professional accomplishments and education. If you have the latter, there is nothing wrong with including them; but what God has done in your life is more important.

Your topics should be appropriate for as broad a group of people as possible. For example, if you want to write about surviving cancer, don't limit your speaking audience to victims of cancer and their families. Broaden your topic to dealing with adversity. Everyone faces difficulties, and most of the experiences you had with cancer can be translated to a general audience.

You can include from one topic up to as many as ten to fifteen. Give each topic a catchy title and write a description in a few sentences of what that presentation includes. Additionally, list what type of group it is appropriate for and how long the speech takes.

Your information sheet should also include your name in a large font across the top or side and a photo, both of which should express your personality and style. If you are creating your first information sheet, you might want to use a preprinted paper with decorative borders or themes. They are a cost-effective way to create an attractive piece. Select the paper that fits you the best and print the text using an ink jet, laser printer, or copier. Three companies we recommend through CLASS for preprinted paper are Paper Direct (800-A-PAPERS), Idea Art (800-433-2278), and Paper Showcase (800-287-8163). You can receive samples of some of our speakers' information sheets through CLASS and check out their content through the CLASS web site at www.classervice.com.

Spread the Word

Once you have your information sheet, you need to get it into the hands of people who might want to hire you. There are several ways to go about doing this.

Include it in your Christmas card along with a note telling your friends this is what you are doing now and that if their Bible study teacher needs someone to fill in or their church needs a speaker, they should think of you. Ask your friends to give your information sheet to their pastors, women's ministry directors, and/or Bible study teachers.

Ask your pastor, assuming he is in support of your ministry, to send a letter to fellow ministers. Most pastors have friends all over the country with whom they went to seminary. They know the other pastors in their denomination and the local group of pastors who may be from different denominations.

Most pastors will not have time to do this for you if you expect them to do all the work. Offer to create the cover letter introducing you (allow him to review it and make changes as necessary), print it on church letterhead, address the envelopes, and pay for the postage yourself. By doing so, you make it easy for your pastor to help you. When the letter of introduction comes from the pastor to his friends, it will be opened. If you send letters to unknown persons at all the churches in your community, the vast majority will end up in the trash and be a waste of time and money.

Another way to generate speaking contacts is to check the local paper for upcoming events that feature speakers. If your topic can be presented to a secular audience, look in the business section (or wherever your local paper lists club and business meetings) for the listings of this week's events. If your topic is appropriate for a Christian audience, check in the religion section, usually included in the Saturday paper, for events happening that week. If the listing mentions a speaker, you know that group utilizes speakers.

Track the listings for several weeks so you can be aware of groups and churches that use speakers. Call the contact number in the listing. Ask for the name and number of the program chairman and then contact that person to let him or her know you are interested in speaking to that group. The chairman will usually ask you to send your information sheet.

Whether you get the contacts through your own network of friends, your pastor, or your research into local events, you will want to follow-up on the materials you send out to see if the contact person has questions or needs additional information or tapes of your speaking. Call once or twice, but don't make a pest of yourself.

This process will allow you to plant the seeds or knock on the doors that let people know you are available. If this is where God wants you, He will provide the increase; the bookings will begin to happen. As you speak and touch people's lives, you will get additional invitations to speak.

As previously mentioned, these speaking engagements are of great interest to publishers as they decide whether or not to publish your work. If you are already published, speaking is important to both you and the publisher as it sells books. If your book sells well, the publisher will be interested in your next book.

You certainly didn't write the book just for your own personal gratification. You wrote it because you believe God has given you a message you want others to hear, and they need to hear. If that is the case, you want the book to get into the hands of as many people as possible. It will not change lives sitting in your garage or in the publisher's warehouse.

Today there are so many books on the market that just writing them and getting them published does not insure they will be in the bookstores. In most cases, the public will never know about your book unless you are out there speaking on that topic and letting people know the book exists. Speaking and writing go together like a hand in a glove.

Market Your Books

When you go to a speaking engagement, be sure to take a selection of your books with you. If you have audio tapes or mention books by other authors, you can include them on your book table as well. As you are speaking, mention your book as a part of your content, not as an advertisement.

You might read a short section from your book. You might casually say, "If you would like more information on this topic, it's in my book." At appropriate times, hold the book up once or twice during your presentation. Doing this lets your audience know you have a book and it is available on site. When you follow this procedure, whether the book is yours or written by another author, you will usually sell one book for every ten people in the audience.

"One for every ten?" you might ask. Yes, that is a realistic figure. Some groups will buy more, so if you are driving, you might want to take a few extra copies. Kathy Collard Miller tells about her first speaking engagement after her first book was released in 1984. There were going to be twenty-five women there. She eagerly anticipated that they would each want a book and most likely want one or two for their friends, so she took about forty books, set them all up, and was discouraged and embarrassed when she only sold two. Now, as the author of over thirty books, Kathy has a much more realistic expectation of what her audience will buy. But she has discovered that the more books she has available on the book table, the more books the audience buys.

A sale of two books doesn't sound like it will make much difference; but as you speak more and more and to larger and larger groups, the numbers add up. The more books you sell, the more people your work is helping. Additionally, bookstores report that when an author has been to a community, they see an increase in the sales of that author's books. The sales show your publisher there is an interest in your work. They help you financially, too, as most speakers do better in their product sales than they do in fees.

Whether you are already published, or are trying to get published, make speaking a part of the package as speaking and writing really do go together like a hand in a glove.

MARITA LITTAUER has been speaking professionally for over twenty years. She is the author of eight books including *Personality Puzzle*, *Getting Along With Almost Anybody*, and *Talking So People Will Listen*. She is the president of CLASServices Inc., an organization that provides resources, training, and promotion for Christian speakers, authors, and publishers. Since 1981, the CLASSeminars have trained thousands of men and women in speaking and writing skills. The CLASS Reunion is held each year in conjunction with the Christian Booksellers Association convention and offers speakers who are ready to be published an opportunity to meet face to face with a variety of publishers regarding their manuscripts. For more information on any of CLASServices' programs, call 800-433-6633 or visit their Web site at www.classervices.com.

Order Form

Postal orders:
ACW Press, 5501 N. 7th Ave., Suite 502, Phoenix, AZ 85013

Credit Card orders: (800) 931-BOOK (2665)
Visa and Mastercard accepted.

Please send A *Complete Guide to Writing for Publication* to:

Name:____

Address:______________________________________

City:________________________ State: ___________

Zip: _________________

Telephone: (   ) ______________________

Book Price: $15.00 in U.S. dollars.

Sales Tax: Please add 6.85% for books shipped to an Arizona address.

Shipping: $4.00 for the first book and $1.00 for each additional book to cover shipping and handling within US, Canada, and Mexico. International orders add $6.00 for the first book and $2.00 for each additional book.

Quantity Discounts Available - Please call for information
(602) 336-8910